SOLD OUT WARNING

HAS OUR ~~NATION~~ Government SOLD
ITS SOUL FOR
TECHNOLOGY?

To Greg
Ps: 91
No Fear

Ronnie McMullen

RONNIE McMULLEN

ACKNOWLEDGEMENTS

This book was a mountain to climb, and I believe all mountains have peaks. There were many people who helped me obtain this peak. I thank the Lord Jesus first for giving me the courage to finish the task. I thank my wife and family for giving me up to a project that took so much time. Thanks to my editors for their sacrifice and excellent attitude in their editing efforts. I couldn't have done it without you. I thank Michael Janiczek for his professionalism and his patience. We did take the oath never to use Microsoft Works again!

I want to give thanks to a true warrior, William Branton, author of the Dulce Wars, for his courage and faith and deep research into a phenomenon of aliens/fallen ones that far surpasses anyone I know. I also want to thank Gary Schultz who helped flame the fire that was already there. He brought laughter and strength when I needed it most. I thank Corina Saebels for her sacrifice and boldness in carrying the truth to those who do not know. Corina, you're great!

I would also like to close with thanking all of those who know the truth, and are bold enough to tell it to a world that is clueless. God's speed to you!

FOREWORD

As a scientist, I know how critical it is that words maintain stability to accomplish intended results. Could disaster be very far away if yesterday's *hydrochloric acid* was newly and arbitrarily labeled *water*? And so it is with words relating to significant concepts.

Pontius Pilate struggled with the meaning of the word *truth*. A considerable number in our generation regard word definitions as negotiable and thus would echo Pilate's confusion regarding truth. Yet, *truth* is central to the analysis in this volume by Ronnie McMullen. Fortunately, the Scriptures come to our aid to dispel confusion. We are informed by the apostle John in John 1:14 that the Word (Jesus Christ) was full of grace and *truth*. And as Mr. McMullen reminds us, Jesus Christ stated in John 14:6, "I am the way, the *truth*, and the life…" We therefore know that the truth is inseparable from the truth of Jesus Christ.

One of the most controversial subjects addressed in this book is that of the Nephilim first mentioned in Genesis chapter 6. The early Church believed, as did the Old Testament believers, that the Nephilim could not possibly be the sons of Seth (the Sethite view). This historical and traditional viewpoint is faithfully upheld in this work. That alone makes Mr. McMullen's book a <u>must</u> to own and read.

Mr. McMullen also focuses the reader's attention to secret societies. While they are not always functioning in a conspiratorial mode, they are inherently engineered to do so. They oft times present a public persona of administering good works to society. But a veneer of decency can obscure an unmonitored pursuit of goals oriented toward self-interest at the expense of those outside the group. One is reminded of Christ's harsh rebuke of the Pharisees (a quasi-secret society of the day), whereby He likened them to whited sepulchres full of dead men's bones (Matt. 23:27).

An unbiased examination of the historical record regarding secret societies points to the common thread underlying their proliferation throughout the ages, and that is their continuing dedication to teaching and preserving occult doctrines and philosophies. A spotlight is essential on these groups, and Mr. McMullen does a stellar job with this subject. An important distinction is made between the common "foot soldiers" and their overlords in the secret societies, which call themselves the *adepts*. They indeed are adept at deception, even to the point of deceiving their own membership at large about their actual beliefs and symbolism. These core groups are collectively known as the *Illuminati*, which name aptly describes the actual source of their enlightenment—Lucifer, who is not such a bad fellow in their scheme of things.

It is this inner elite which is behind the sinister machinations which are the subject of a great deal of this book. Mr. McMullen points out that Freemasonic societies in particular are the most prominent modern power centers of the sundry secret societies in existence today that are manipulating major world events behind the curtain, away from public view.

Mr. McMullen identifies by what means the *Illuminati* has been implementing their goal of bringing a unification of mankind, economically, politically and spiritually. They call their end desire the New World Order. The term *globalism* is an overarching synonym for the current system in place being deployed toward reaching this objective. While their low-rung adherents probably pursue this dream without malice, the top-tiered power-brokers seek to forcibly fulfill the mandate of preparing the world for their false christ. Globalism is one means by which economic and political power is being concentrated in fewer hands.

The progress to date by a tiny but furtive Luciferian elite in having successfully molded planetary agenda to their will and long range objectives has finally gained an ascendancy making them—especially at this late hour—the most serious threat to all of humankind.

The aliens are the architects of their own secrecy. The aliens are here . . . the evil aliens. Now they have joined forces with, thereby adding an entirely new scope and dimension to, the *Illuminati*. That's the bad news. Are there good aliens? We can't be sure. So far I've not heard of any *sold out aliens for Christ*.

I have taken the opportunity to read numerous books covering the subjects contained in this book. Most of these authors sidestep the critical spiritual insights provided through proper understanding of the Scriptures. Other authors obtain their "insights" from sources that could be viewed kindly as dubious at best. Few, it seems, are able to cut through the morass of confusion and arrive at a sound analysis. Mr. McMullen fits into the latter category, as he rightly divides the word of truth to ascertain the spiritual basis for these remarkable events and phenomena. Kudos to Mr. McMullen for bringing obscure facts to light in this immensely informative and important addition to books on these history-changing subjects. His book reverberates with crucial insights for our time.

Gary E. Schultz

TABLE OF CONTENTS

INTRODUCTION

Everything of integrity must start with five simple letters. T -R -U- T -H. The question is, what is truth? Who even tells the truth anymore? In fact, truth is buried while lies are given free of charge. Why does truth cost us in this life? Why does one have to work overtime or have to sacrifice to even get to five little letters of absolute importance? Truth. Is it that easy to lie? Sure it is. In fact, if you can lie and sell it as truth, you've arrived. Or have you? Arrived at what? A dead end. A pile of dung. There is one thing for certain, you can take the truth and blow it up, shoot it, run over it, burn it, throw it off a cliff, bury it, or even deny it, but it will still stand.

This book, that I was reluctant to write, is about the truth. It is the truth as I believe it. Is it possible that my truth as I believe may not be your truth as you believe it? The Lord Jesus was instrumental in letting me write this book, giving me the courage to go forth and making the distribution of this book possible however He sees fit.

The truth as you know it could change by seeing divine truth cancel out false truth. We as a nation are being taught to believe an untruth. In fact, Webster's dictionary defines the word deceive, as to cause to believe an untruth. Are we really being taught to believe an untruth? Has it ever occurred to you that our technology is advancing at such a rate of speed that it seems unreal? Now I'm not one to be a stick in the mud, but sometimes the technology advances so fast it scares me. Maybe because I have not understood it and anything people don't understand they tend to fear. No one likes to fear. Fear can intimidate and fear can paralyze. Both intimidation and paralysis can cause one to fall in a trap or snare and be controlled. Lions are considered to be Kings of the jungle. In this case King would refer to a ruler. In Africa, there are those that fear lions, and those that hunt lions. Lion hunters conquer their own fear so that they can hunt the lion that preys on the sheep. The lion hunter cannot focus on the lion, but must focus on the hunt. The hunt is the mandate for everyone's safety. I am a hunter. A hunter for truth, and I want that key to enter into another world filled with peace and joy, because finding the truth brings life and safety. The word truth is one of the words that characterize Jesus. Jesus states: *"I am the Way, the Truth, and the Life, No one comes to the Father except through Me"*. This is the key and entrance into another world, the world of heaven. When hunting for the "truth" armor must be worn. Jesus Christ is our armor and holds the key to truth. He is the truth.

There must be truth in the alien conspiracy and someone created these life forms. Who? I want to remind you, the word conspire means to plan secretly an unlawful act; to plot. Why is the alien phenomenon such a big secret? If it was good, fruitful, and advantageous, why is its truth not brought to light? Shhhshshsh. Our government seems to be better about secrets than they are about shepherding the country. Too bad for us. Six men seeking the truth have either been killed in unusual deaths, or critically injured. This was an act done in intimidation to silence them speaking out the truth.

Investigative Reporter: Danny Casolaro
Government Engineer and Lecturer: Phillip Schneider
Writer: Jim Keith
Publisher: Ron Bonds
Talk Show Host: William Cooper
Writer: William Branton

Now we can call this coincidence or we can call it what it is. Spooky. I have yet to find any book go in to depth in the natural and in the spiritual of the alien threat, not just in this nation of America, but in the whole world. I once received an e-mail from someone who wrote; the "truth" as you know it today may not be the "truth" as you know it tomorrow. Walk in the power of your Lord and be strong and do 'great things'. Steven Spielberg's movie, "War of The Worlds" may not be a truth, or is it?- - - You decide.

The First Chapter

IT ALL STARTS AT THE SEED

I remember at fifteen years old, when I took my first female companion to the movies. I had to be humbled as I was chauffeured in the back of my dad's '74 Nova. We thought it would be fun to see a sci-fi movie that *everyone* in our school was talking about. I wanted to be included in their conversations talking about the latest flick, "Close Encounters Of The Third Kind". This was at a time before directors were as important as actors and actresses. So, Steven Spielberg was not a household name then, as he is today. As the movie began, the anticipation grew inside of me, wondering what I would see on this "big screen" before me. I had to balance my fears that night. The fear of what I might see on the screen, versus the fear of being slapped as I tried to put my arm around my date sitting next to me. The outcome leaned in my favor. My date leaned into me as I put my arm around her. The movie was chilling. Someone or something stole a little boy right out of his house. Worse yet, his mom could not protect or save him from this atrocity. My Lord, this movie was saying we have life forms from somewhere else! Where did these spaceships come from? Who, what, where? I thought I would have to peel my date off of me because she was so afraid... She was very afraid.

Everything starts as a seed. A seed planted takes root and grows into a huge plant. Many of today's population has had a seed planted long ago and their belief system is based off of that seed. The Bible talks about wheat and tares. Wheat represents good seed, while tares represent bad or false seed. Tares look a lot like wheat and grow up in the fields with wheat. Most of the time you don't know which is which, until the harvest.

9

Then, the wheat and tares are separated and put in their designated places. We can use the parable of wheat and tares to represent good and bad people; but could it mean something much deeper? The Bible is a mystery to those who hunt for *truth* on a daily basis. Could Jesus have been saying something else with the wheat and tares parable? Could a perverted seed be living amongst us in and on this earth? And if so, who is responsible? How did it happen? Why? Why does the government cover up, hide, and deceive every time there is a UFO sighting, or downed spacecraft with eyewitnesses? What is the truth and where can one find out about these highly classified top-secret events?

I have wondered myself many, many times; could this all be a precursor to a much larger event in the future? An event so huge, so sinister, that it deceives close to all the population? Is it a deception? Maybe it is a very large deception... A Grand Deception. These questions and more will hopefully be answered in the pages of this book. But please be reminded, I am not a man with a doctorate. I have not been educated by this world to its highest levels. I am just a man who knows something is wrong. Very wrong. I have researched so my questions could be answered. Hopefully my answers will help you.

Why do the huge mega-ministries push a pre-tribulation rapture to the people of the United States? Other countries don't believe in rapture before persecution. The early church believed that we would go through suffering before Jesus' return. Could there be another agenda the world is not seeing? Now, we even have President Bush masquerading as a rapture man behind a veil of *false prayer*. Again, I'll take you back in time to why we are where we are today. It's about the seed. It provoked God to destroy the earth's population in the days of Noah. I believe God once again is being provoked to destroy the earth's population. Why, you ask? Because of the seed. The perverted seed.

To understand the alien phenomenon you must first understand the so-called alien. Some call them ET's, which stands for extra-terrestrial. Some call them EB's, which means extra-terrestrial biological entities. We must also understand where they come from and what they really are. Who made these other life forms? I believe this huge paint by number picture is starting to show its image. Again... I am always going to tell you what I believe... God the Father is the Creator of the heavens and the earth and everything in it.

Let's start in the beginning..... I must grab truth from the best-selling book of all times. It is also one of the oldest books of all time. You may not believe the Bible to be truth, but I believe it is. I don't want to sound too preachy or too religious; but I must stand on what I believe. In Genesis 1:1 it states, *"In the beginning, God created the heaven and the earth."* Verse 2, *"and the earth was without form, and void; and darkness was upon the face of the deep. And the spirit of God moved upon the face of the waters."* Verse 3, *"and God said let there be light, and there was light."* Now many people of this world have a problem with verse one and verse three. Verse one, *"God created heaven and earth,"* and verse three, *"and God said, let there be light."* People don't have a problem with God creating light, they have a problem with *God said.* So the big problem of our world is... *creation* and *God said.* How interesting that many have difficulty with two thirds of the first three verses of the Bible. Could it be a coincidence in the last book of the Bible, Revelation Chapter 8, that the Lord God is going to send fire and destroy one third of the earth's surface and allow one third of the earth's water supply to be contaminated? One third fire + one third water contamination = two thirds of a problem on earth. Strange? Coincidence? Or parallel? So why are those two verses so important to humanity? Again I'll say, it all starts at the seed. *Creation*, and *God said.* If the Bible is truth, then the Lord God is the supreme ruler over all creation. If these verses are a lie, then someone else is the supreme ruler over all creation. Satan knows this. He knows the Bible better than anyone on the face of the earth from past to present. Satan is not just going to go back a few years and then start altering truths. He is going to try to mess with the foundations of creation. Because if he is not caught he can destroy and deceive the people of this earth so that they will spend eternity in hell with him.

As soon as Satan fell from heaven, the war began. The Lord God is Spirit as well as Truth. That means that this war is spiritual. Always has been, always will be. All wars are spiritual, do your homework. Adolf

Hitler thought he was not only going to be the ruler over Germany, but the ruler over the world. When you talk about ruling a world, you talk about being in control. Serving the Lord God, Jehovah Elohim, or Satan, Lucifer. Religion is defined as worshipping a deity. Maybe you are starting to see that you are smack dab in the middle of a huge mega religious war. And all the wars on this earth might be seen as little battles, using humans against humans for the fight of control. I truly believe these little battles as I call them, are leading to a huge war that is building in heaven and on earth. Remember verse one of Genesis? *In the beginning God created the heaven and earth.* Satan didn't create the earth, he couldn't. Lucifer cannot create anything. But he is a master at duplicating, lying, and deceiving. Remember if you can create a counterfeit currency, it is only a third of the crime. You must lie about the money being real then use it to deceive the people in exchange to gain the control of the transaction. They must believe it is real. Then the crime is complete. Satan must convince us of the lie that God did *not* create us. If we can believe this lie then when the Grand Deception comes, the crime of all time will be complete. The crime of taking millions or billions of people straight to hell. Tragedy.

Satan has been perverting the seed with lies and deception since the beginning. If he is barred from heaven, you can be assured he wants you to suffer with him. I want to clear up some false teachings that are floating around about Eve in Genesis. This has to do with the question did Eve sleep with the serpent or snake in the Garden of Eden? Because once again this has to do with the seed. You might be appalled that I could even mention the possibility of Eve having intercourse with a snake. How disgusting to even think such a thing! But oddly enough, information junkies believe that in the Garden of Eden when the serpent tempted Eve, that the two of them had intercourse. These information hounds believe that the serpent raped Eve. Is this true, or just another altercation of the truth? Here is a point that this world must remember: a truth + a lie = a lie. A lie + a truth = a lie. A lie + a lie = a lie. Truth stands by itself, all alone. And truth needs no help from anything or anyone to be absolute. I have learned many things in my research and that is that people: read, think, meditate, perceive, calculate... and then believe. The perception is the key factor in what your personal belief system dictates. Many men and women are in prison unjustly because twelve people perceived that they were guilty of the crime committed. But, if the defense attorney did not present his facts or truths correctly, he or she will be charged with a crime they did not commit.

May I present the facts and truths with Adam's wife Eve. In Genesis 3:1 it says; " *Now the serpent was more subtle than any beast of the field which the Lord God had made.*" That statement connotes that the Lord God made everything *including the serpent*. It also states that the serpent was more sly or clever than the rest. Let's go on. *And he said to the woman, "Yea, has God said, you shall not eat of every tree of the garden?"* Before we hear Eve's reply we need to know the depth of this question proposed to Eve. "*Yea, has God said?*" You see, the serpent knew about the special tree in the midst of the garden. He was interrogating Eve for her information and what her plans were about that tree of the knowledge of good and evil. Remember the two big problems of this world; *creation* and *God said*. The serpent opened his interrogation with; "*Yea, has God said?*" He was setting the *seed* for Eve to challenge God. This is where we find the seed planted for the tree of rebellion. The true meaning for rebellion is: resistance to authority. Now there is something else I want to point out about the conversation between the serpent and Eve. Did you take notice that Eve was fearful, frightened, or afraid of the serpent? The answer is "NO". There was no fear, no guilt, and no shame. Now let's go back to the serpent's interrogation of what Eve was told by God. Verse two, "*And the woman said to the serpent, we may eat of the fruit of the trees of the garden: but of the fruit of the tree which is in the midst of the garden, God has said, you shall not eat of it, neither shall you touch it, lest you die.*" Verse four, "*Now the serpent said to the woman, you shall not surely die.*" This is a direct contradiction to what God said. Since the Lord God has made everything including the serpent, you can see where the serpent stands. He stands on rebellion, resistant to God's authority. God said versus serpent said. It's kind of interesting that if you're not doing what God says, you're automatically doing what the serpent says. Now here's where the story gets wild. Verse five says, *"For God does know in the day you eat thereof, then your eyes shall be opened and you shall be as gods knowing good and evil."* Now imagine that. We will be as gods. I think this is the carrot to all mankind to be in power and control and to masquerade as a little god. Now here's where the story smoothes out. Verse six, *" And when the woman saw that the tree was good for food, and that it was pleasant to the eyes, and a tree to be desired to make one wise, she took of the fruit thereof, and did eat, and gave also to her husband with her; and he did eat. "* Let me show you how I perceive that verse and translate it in today's language. When the woman justified that the tree was food, and saw nothing wrong with it, and that this tree would give her power from knowledge, she took the fruit and ate it. There are always consequences for mistakes. This mistake, this sin, this mess up, wasn't just for that time, but changed the course of history throughout all generations. One must study the past to know where we'll be in the future. Now we come down a few verses and we find some interesting facts that show where we are in today's timeline. First of all, God goes right to Adam and asks...*"Where are you?* Verse ten, *"And he said, I heard your voice in the garden and I was afraid, because I was naked, and I hid myself."* This is the first mention of fear in the Bible. I think it is ironic that fear comes right after having an encounter with the serpent. (*Maybe this is a close encounter of the first kind.*) Is this a snake? Is this a serpent? Let's go to the truth so no one exits here and goes into a mystery of theories and lies. Verse thirteen, *"And the Lord God said to the woman, what is this that you've done? And the woman said, the serpent beguiled me, and I did eat."* Beguiled is a meaning for tricked or deceived. Some scholars have twisted the meaning for this word to mean rape, thus implying that the serpent had intercourse with Eve and raped her. Not so! I'll prove this on two accounts. First: beguile in the Hebrew means nasha, which means to lead astray mentally or seduce morally. I need you to remember this meaning because I'm going to tie this into fact later with alien abductions.

Let's talk about this serpent in the garden that is mentally disturbing Eve and causing her to go against God. Was the serpent a snake, or was he something else? The answer starts in verse fourteen, *"And the Lord God said to the serpent, because you have done this, you are cursed above all cattle, and above every beast of the field; upon your belly shall you go and dust shall you eat all the days of your life."* Part of this verse curses the serpent and tells him he is now going to be upon his belly. Are we to believe that this serpent or snake was standing before this curse? Do you think it odd that Eve is talking to a snake? I have never in my entire life talked to a snake or serpent that has spoken back to me. We might refer to a person as acting like a snake, but this usually means we don't trust them or that the person has no integrity. It does not mean that this person has scales and a forked tongue. But God said this was a serpent, a snake.

There have been sightings today of reptilians being seen near entrances to mountain ranges and these creatures look to be half-man/half-reptile. This may be very hard to swallow, but I would ask you to consider why people would make up this story; and why there have been sightings by various people who have no connection with each other seeing the same reptile-man looking creature? Most of these sightings are near government underground installations and these reptilians guard their entrance. I don't want to lose you, but facts are facts. Men die reporting on these facts, digging into the unknown and bringing light to the darkness. There have been hidden secrets for thousands of years and the Lord God Most High promises He will bring light to the darkness. I do not believe these reptilians are Satan, I believe they are demons (*real*) that answer to Satan. They are not ghost-like, made-up, demon spirits that float around saying, *"BOO."* Instead they are real live demonic reptile, human-like subjects that are here for a purpose and a mission. Their orders must be carried out or they will be greatly punished by their master. Believe me, he is not full of grace, mercy, peace, and love. Where do you think torture began? Some evil man like Hitler, or Stalin, who just had a taste for the evil theater? No, just as Eve was mentally tempted to go against God and enter into darkness, the same evil is mentally transported to those who have no reverence or submission to the Lord God Most High. Remember, it's a spiritual war out there and you're in the middle. If people are not shown the truth, many, many, many, will be led into darkness by way of the Grand Deception.

Since the truth is not readily available on every street corner, it paints a picture that those who carry the truth are straight out of the mental ward, and need to be put away for their crazy beliefs. Are you aware that when Adolf Hitler was rising to power people liked him? But after he started showing his true colors, they started to see who he really was and it was too late.

I want to show you just a couple more wild similarities and see if I can get your eyebrows to rise. It is not my intention to be on the New York Times best selling book list for months at a time. I am a man just like you who has a taste for the truth. A man who has found some answers for people's questions to the unknown. A man who knows that something very evil and dark is coming in the near future.

A man who wants to warn the people of a Grand Deception that will cause people to die not just one death, but two. A natural death, followed by a spiritual death. Here are those hair-raising similarities: The Lord God said, *"You will be cursed above all cattle and above every beast of the field."* Ponder this... Did you know that there are thousands of reported cattle mutilations near UFO sightings around the world? Not horses, rabbits, dogs, or cats, but cattle. And what is the first animal that God says the serpent is cursed above? Cattle. What do the people in India worship? Cattle. Hmmm. If you think that is creepy, listen to this: Snakes have a tongue that splits at the end. It is known as a "forked tongue". The American Indians were implying that the man that speaks with a "forked tongue" is one who lies, or changes his story. No truth, no integrity. In the Bible this is called being double-minded and God strongly warns us against being double-minded. Could the "forked tongue" and double-minded thought be a parallel? If Eve was mentally tempted, that means that the enemy was speaking to her mind to get her off the road or path she was on (*obedience*). This might be called the "fork in the road". God said, or serpent said? Coincidence? Parallel? Mind-boggling?... You decide. Where is your foundation?

You may be healthy in your body and work out daily, but I assure you it won't save you in this spiritual war. The mind is a beautiful thing, and it must be protected by a belief system that measures "in truth". Ephesians 6:17 says, *"Take the helmet of Salvation and the Sword of the Spirit, which is the Word of God."* There are three chunks of meat for you to chew on before we go on to the next Chapter. Verse 17 in Ephesians is a good nugget. If we are to believe that this serpent or serpents are real today, they will try to speak and communicate to us through our minds (*telepathically*). Why does God refer to His Salvation as being a helmet? To protect the mind. These demon/reptile/human things have spirit in them. And trust me, it's not Holy. God says in the same verse to take the <u>Sword</u> (*weapon*) of the *Holy* Spirit, which is the Word of God. Remember the two big problems of the earth? *Creation* and *God said*. So, that sword of protection is: *God Said*. It's your choice. And speaking of *God said*, I have one more place in the Bible to show you before we go on to the next Chapter. Now remember, the world has a problem with two things, *God said* and *Creation*. Remember the Ten Commandments? Those ten orders that God said you should obey? If one wants to do the wrong thing, follow your own plan, you're not going to glance at ten rules to follow and obey. Your *mind* is already made up to rebel. Therefore, maybe you might just miss a clue to the future that is sitting right in front of you. A future that was foretold

> **The mind is a beautiful thing, and it must be protected by a belief system that measures "in truth".**

thousands of years before it would happen. The clue is found in Exodus 20:3-5, *"You shall have no other gods before Me."* We all understand that. People may not like to obey that command, but they do understand it. *"You shall not make to you any graven image, or any likeness of any thing that is in Heaven above, or that is in the earth beneath, or that is in the water under the earth."* Before we go to verse five, did you get the clue? Is there more to worry about than flying discs from outer space? Are we being warned through the Bible that there is something under the surface of the earth? Something that might want to be a god? Something so deep that it could be found under the water under the earth? Talk about going deep! Hold on... we're not finished. Verse five: *"You shall not bow down yourself to them, nor serve them: For I the Lord your God am a jealous God, visiting the iniquity of the fathers upon the children to the third and fourth generation of them that hate Me."* Do you find it strange that the Lord God warns us not to bow to *THEM*? Who in the world are *THEM*? He also warns not to serve them for He is a jealous God. This would imply that *THEM* want to be seen as gods. And here is a valid question, why is God visiting the iniquity of the fathers upon the children to the third and fourth generations of them that hate Him? Is something wrong with the third and fourth generations? Do those generations have a problem in the code? Moral code, genetic code? Is the word *THEM* referring to the same them that crashed at Roswell, New Mexico? Is it the same *THEM* that the governments around the world keep secret to all mankind? And maybe there is a huge clue to where they live. Not in outer space, but down deep under the earth's crust where it's warm. Very warm.

And once again, Eve did not have intercourse with the serpent. Genesis 4:1, *"And Adam knew Eve his wife; and she conceived and bore Cain, and said, 'I have gotten a man from the Lord."* Verse two. *"And she again bore his brother Abel. And Abel was a keeper of the sheep, but Cain was a tiller of the ground."* The reason we must understand this foundation is so that there are no lies in the genealogy of Jesus. For if the genealogy of Jesus is contaminated, He would not be the Truth.

> **For if the genealogy of Jesus is contaminated, He would not be the Truth.**

The Bible tells us that Jesus is the Way, the Truth, and the Life. We now know that this genealogy is pure. This fact is most upsetting to Satan. If Satan tried to take over this world in a red suit with horns, carrying a fiery pitchfork, not many would follow him. But what if a being, or beings, showed up with technology light years ahead of modern day? Is this a carrot... or a ...?

�

Ronnie McMullen

The Second Chapter

I Don't Believe It, Not For A Second

Little green men in rubber suits wandering around, flying saucers and laser beams are concepts that many find hard to believe. People in this world will do anything for five minutes of fame. Con artists and hoaxes have filled our world's closet for centuries. Some do it for fame, some do it for money, and some do it for the enjoyment of just doing it. However you look at it, when deceit, lies, and trickery are surrounding you, it can be very hard to find the truth.

In the case of Travis Walton it was very hard to find the truth. On November 5th, 1975, Travis Walton was allegedly abducted by a UFO in the Sitgreaves National Forest near Snowflake, Arizona. A twenty-two year old logger traveling with six fellow employees saw a spaceship hovering over a pile of cut lumber in a clearing. So as the story is told, Walton jumped out of the truck and ran toward the ship.

> **However you look at it, when deceit, lies, and trickery are surrounding you, it can be very hard to find the truth.**

Suddenly, the spaceship beamed a flash of blue-green light that knocked him back ten feet. This account was witnessed by Walton's friend and employer, Mike Rogers. In a full -fledged panic, Rogers sped off leaving Travis alone at the sight of this alien ship. Rogers then drove to a small town called Heber, the closest to the work site, and contacted Under-Sheriff Ellison and gave his story. Ellison then contacted Navajo County

Sheriff Marlin Gillespie, and his deputy Kenneth Coplan. Ellison, Gillespie, Coplan, Rogers and two other crewmembers returned to the site and searched well into the night for Walton. He was not to be found.

Five days later Travis Walton reappeared at a gas station in Heber. On March 12, 1993, "Fire in The Sky" opened in theatres across America. The movie was based on Travis Walton's experience with a UFO abduction. Or was it a twisted Hollywood story based on a real hoax?

Philip J. Klass, chairman of CSICOP's UFO subcommittee investigated the Walton case immediately after it happened. Mr. Klass in his study of Walton's story would later come to the conclusion that he found significant evidence of gross deception.

Was the script writer Tracy Torme, who also wrote CBS's miniseries on alien abductions, "Intruders", a screen writer that had an agenda to move the public toward believing in alien abductions? Or was this scriptwriter just looking for box office thrills? You must be the judge. As for Travis Walton, he has had interviews with CNBC's Tom Snyder Show, Larry King Live, Hard Copy, and Fox's Sightings Show.

> **Truth is a rare commodity. It is more precious than gold.**

Was Travis Walton abducted and kept for five days only to find a mark on his arm after his return? Was this a man who was looking for five minutes of fame, or was Travis telling the truth and the media mongrels just twisted it?

Maybe he wanted some pocket money. Stories like this seem only to confuse people. And maybe that's why we know this story from our friendly media.

Truth is a rare commodity. It is more precious than gold. You will hear some say, "I have to see it before I believe it." That saying became a way of life. Why? Because people have lied, cheated, and tricked others for centuries. So if we see it right before our eyes we will believe it. So why not have some situations happen right before our eyes? I mean, let's face the facts, if we see it, we will believe it.

This information of other life forms can't be dumped on us all at once. They must acquaint us a little bit at a time, so we don't freak out or die of shock or fear. I have an idea, let's go to the movies... or how about some radio theater? Let's not bring the public straight to the truth, but let their eyes see an imitation of the truth. All people (male and female) are visual. When people see something with their eyes, it has quite an effect on them. We'll call this... visual effects.

Visual effects have enhanced our belief of the imitation while watching the big screen for years. What you see on the screen is not what is really being filmed. Visual effects have become so advanced that you're not sure what you are really viewing. Is it reality or imitation? Visual effects play a major role in the movie business. If the producers and directors make you believe what you saw is real, then they have truly succeeded. In fact, if the producers and directors can make you believe that what you saw was partial reality, they have succeeded. The term, "keep you guessing", comes to mind. This in fact puts a spin of control on the public. Major media from news to films have controlled and manipulated the public for many years, guiding and directing their beliefs to a One World, unity driven agenda. The New World Order is such a big part of this alien/fallen angel agenda. Here is a quote from the Sauder Zone Website that explains a piece of the history of the formation of the New World Order.

"As World War II was drawing to a close and General George Patton was making his deadly push into the heart of Europe in pursuit of Nazi forces who were beginning to realize that their fascist empire was about to crumble –or so it seemed –a counter-measure was put into effect by deep-level agents of the Nazi S.S. This bold and brazen plan was to effect not only an escape of the inner core of the Nazi S.S. but also to implement an infiltration of the United States' military-industrial establishment using Nazi S.S. 5th column agents in America who would be instructed to blend-in with the population and coordinate their corporate armies in preparation for a future attempt to take control of the American government from within!

So, how were the Nazi's able to infiltrate the heart of American Intelligence without giving themselves away? They would have to have received backing from a very powerful organization already operating within the confines of the American Republic. The only thing more powerful than the American government itself, the Nazis discovered, were the multi-billion-dollar corporate empires which had a considerable influence on the American political system behind-the-scenes. One of the most powerful of these financial empires had put Dwight D. Eisenhower into the presidency, as well as one of their own family members into the Vice Presidency. This financial empire was none other than the ROCKEFELLER FOUNDATION. This foundation had a great deal of influence in the media and, in turn, in manipulating public opinion in favor of their own political agendas.

According to the well-known International economist Dr. Antony Sutton, the Rockefellers not only helped to finance the Nazi Empire –the Rockefellers being long-time members of Bavarian-German secret societies that were determined to rule the world by establishing a totalitarian 'New World Order' –but their STANDARD [EXXON] OIL company had literally provided the 'fuel' for the Nazi War machine's conquest of Europe.

Nelson Rockefeller (who was later manipulated into the Vice Presidency) initially brought 3000 crack Nazi S.S. agents into the United States and gave them new identities and positions within their Military-Industrial Establishment. This super-secret operation was called PROJECT PAPERCLIP. Also, several former Nazi scientists from the Peenemunde Aerodynamics Institute which built the 'V-1' and 'V-2' rockets which reigned terror upon England were placed in positions of influence within these corporate/military establishments as well.

The UNITED NATIONS ORGANIZATION [NOW] was initially created by the Bavarian secret orders (or the Bavarian Empire) and is ultimately being run from Bavaria, Germany – although they will never admit to this. Former U.N. Secretary General Kurt Waldheim, an Austrian, has been accused by many of being an undercover Nazi war criminal. He was allegedly one of several Nazi infiltrators who helped form the 'unofficial' genocidal policies of the UNITED NATIONS ORGANIZATION. The Genocidal and Population Control plans of the United Nations are not too difficult to document. The U.N. N.W.O. (UNITED NATIONS NEW

WORLD ORDER) also plans to foment anarchy and race riots in America in preparation for the implementation of Executive Orders which will be used to establish martial law and the presence of a UNITED NATIONS "peace keeping force". They will use the excuse that since "we" have sent "peace keepers" to other countries, we in America are not exempt from U.N. intervention in a time of internal instability. However, these U.N. 'Blue Helmets', once they have established their presence, WILL NEVER LEAVE willingly. Instead they will be used to force Americans to conform to the fascist Bavarian "New World Order" via its "Trojan horse", which is known today as the UNITED NATIONS ORGANIZATION or U.N.O.

Now before you accuse me of suffering from paranoid delusions, I would CHALLENGE you to read this entire series of files, and THEN you can accuse me of paranoid schizophrenia if you wish...

When and if a "U.N. Police Action" is taken against America, the first order of business will be to confiscate all personal weapons (take away the right to bear arms – in fact the Gun Control Act of 1968 was lifted in its entirety from the Nazi Weapons Law of 1938, which was supposed to curb "gang activity" between Nazi and Communist Party thugs); outlaw all non-sanctioned religious activities (remove freedom of worship – or initiate an "inquisition" against all religions that are not approved by the "New World Order"); and confiscate all two-way communications devices such as computers, telephones, fax machines, etc. (disabling freedom of speech – of assembly, free expression, etc. You doubt that such Executive Orders for "Emergency" contingencies are on the books? Then read the concluding files in this series. Better yet, read all the files in order and you'll get a remarkable overview of what is taking place in this world. Remember, knowledge is power and power is protection. Wol.).

These three foundational freedoms, as well as the rest of the BILL OF RIGHTS, will be eliminated if these enemies of freedom and justice have their way. 'Dissenters' will either be shot on site or will be taken to one of the 13 [or more] CONCENTRATION CAMP centers that have been prepared and ARE NOW operational with the United States. Eleven of these have been identified as follows:

Ft. Chaffee, Arkansas;
Ft. Drum, New York;
Ft. Indian Gap, Pennsylvania;
Camp A.P. Hill, Virginia;
Oakdale, California;
Eglin Air Force Bse, Florida;
Vandenberg AFB, California;
Ft. Mc Coy, Wisconsin;
Ft. Benning, Georgia;
Ft. Huachuca, Arizona;
Camp Krome, Florida."

There are many more than these thirteen camps that are listed here. It has been said that there are over 700 of these detention camps just in the United States alone.

Former President George Herbert Walker Bush called for a New World Order in 1992, which would bring all the countries and nations together in unity and "harmony". With that kind of "harmony", (*notice I use this word repeatedly because this is one of the world's leaders favorite terms*) you would only need One World leader or President. No more wars, no more battles... just unity and "harmony" with all people of the world. How sweet! Of course, truth has it that these world leaders are anything but sweet.

A New World Order has been planned since the turn of the century dating back to the early 1900's. Adolf Hitler, who coincidentally was funded by Grandpappy Prescott Bush, was the chosen candidate to bring the world under one "sweet and honest" leader. Somehow, killing and murdering 1.5 million Jews and thousands and thousands of Christians does not sound "sweet and honest". So let's cut to the chase. The selected One World unity-driven leader will not be sweet and honest, he will mirror Adolf Hitler and be a dictator, enslaving billions of people worldwide. What a plan! What a *Grand Plan* devised and birthed by someone of supreme intelligence. Let it be known that someone of a genius-like mind would be selected to be the next Adolf Hitler. This all makes sense... but yet... where would a scheme or plan like this originate from? Someone had to think this up. Someone spoke and put this nasty evil plan in the heads of powerful men who control and manipulate. Who could it be? Could it be the same parallel of Genesis 3:4? ... *"and the serpent said"*. Now, maybe you are starting to see the serpent is not a normal snake as we see in the zoo. Maybe he is more subtle than any beast in the garden. Maybe he is more subtle than any beast or human in the world. Maybe the serpent has a plan to coerce the world leaders into fulfilling his agenda. So here's the *Big, Big Question* has the serpent (alien) talked or communicated with the world leaders?

Remember the mass media I was talking about? They play a huge role in the marketing of the serpent. Now the serpent, or alien, could be quite scary if glanced upon. One would envision a reptile-like man with scales and a snake-like head, and beady black eyes. Coincidentally enough beings like this have reportedly been seen by UFO hunters in remote, rock-like dwellings or cave entrances. If someone changed the look of these serpents, to maybe the likeness of a man in a space suit, or something resembling an astronaut like the Apollo 11 mission; it could be easier for people to digest or accept. If you do your homework and start digging into data reaching back in time, you will come to the shocking truth that the serpent has been communicating with *certain* people for years and years. There is a diabolical plan that some people of this world are involved with, and we are not even aware of it. It is my belief that the serpent or alien has been communicating to world leaders, having them follow a master plan, so that all power will rest on the *one chosen world leader*. Now isn't that bizarre?! The world leaders have put their heads together and come up with a Grand Plan to market the serpent and introduce him to the public. Please understand that I am not saying, nor implying, that our astronauts are space aliens. I am referring to the "Grand" marketing plan. People have to feel comfortable before they will be accepting. So, the plan is to comfort the people with visual effects. You guessed it, the mega-media industry full of money, power, control and deceit.

Have you ever seen a super faith-based, sold out, bold Christian in the film, news or media industry? *NO!* And if there were any, they would be few. There is a unique hush in Hollywood about silently guiding the people to believe and sway with the world leaders' agenda. These Hollywood *powers* are famous, influential and revered by many. They are paid large sums of money to complete a plan, (of course), for the people to believe.

I don't believe the public is truly informed about just how influential the media really is. It started years ago with Orson Welles, and his radio program that shocked the world. In 1938, U.S. actor Orson Welles spoke in his Mercury Theater's radio production of H.G.Well's, "War of The Worlds". This realistic radio production made thousands upon thousands of people panic into thinking that space ships had landed in the United States and that we were at war with outer space. Listeners from everywhere were stricken with absolute fear. Orson would later publicly apologize for all the mishap, fear and confusion. This escapade would later haunt him in his career.

But one might want to dig a little deeper. Who again wrote "War of the Worlds"? British writer and social reformer H.G. Wells. Born 1866, Herbert George Wells wrote such popular science fiction books as; "The Time Machine" (1895), and "The War of The Worlds" (1898). H.G.Wells taught and studied science, while also founding the Fabian Society in 1910. By founding the Fabian Society, he became a social prophet using propaganda to change the world toward socialism. Socialism can very much lead to a dictatorship. And believe me, a dictatorship is a way to bring about a "New World Order". So could we think that Orson Welles, the talented, young aspiring actor was coaxed into a deceptive event that would mark a new time in history? Were world leaders using the media for their purposes of propaganda to bring about a New World Order? Another funny coincidence is that this was at the exact time Adolf Hitler was at the height of his power. In 1938 people did not question news, government, or any other such agencies. Conspiracy was not an option at that time. In those

> **I don't believe the public is truly informed about just how influential the media really is.**

days, most people did not question authority because trust was still a part of the American culture. I'm not saying it was a perfect America at that time, but there was more integrity in our government then, than now.

Is it politically correct of me to say that over sixty-eight years ago there was an elite group of world leaders trying to prepare the world for a "New World Order", and sitting in the seat of power would be *the one world leader*? Now that's power! Coincidentally enough, the summer of 2005 brought us Steven Spielberg and his new and improved "War of The Worlds". Again I would remind you that I don't believe in coincidences. "War of The Worlds" will keep popping up because this is about what is getting ready to happen.

The rumor in the UFO underground research world is that the United States government signed a treaty with the aliens/serpents. In exchange for technology, they would allow the aliens to abduct humans (while turning their heads the other direction) and cattle, as long as a list of adbuctees would be given to the National Security Council. Now this is not the view of the surface UFO research groups. I believe the truth here is that if you play with a snake, you're going to get bit. Unfortunately the aliens, better known as "EBE's", did not tell the truth about the abductees. They only submitted a partial list to the National Security Council. This probably has to do with the EBE's, or serpent/demon's master, whom we are told in the Bible is the father of lies. I will go into greater detail why the serpent/aliens want to abduct the people in the next Chapter.

Since there were thousands of people disappearing, this caused a small panic in our government. Something went wrong and they did not know quite how to handle it. This would also bring about the truth of children being abducted as well. The serpent/alien do not carry sympathy and compassion as humans do. In hell, there is no grace and there is no mercy. Grace and mercy birth compassion.

The big picture here is that a lot of money is being spent to make you believe there are no UFO-alien type extra-terrestrials.

In movies years ago, producers and directors would never write in the script for children to be killed or murdered. The public just would not stand for it, and would reject the film. Thus the movie would flop at the box office. This policy is advancing and has changed. The world is being taught to be less and less compassionate. The question is: where is the world learning this new non-compassionate role from? There are who knows how many children being abducted every year without a trace. And of course we are led to believe that the abductions are carried out by wacko sexually perverted men seeking to rape and kill. Sex offenders have come into a national spotlight and are the sole focus of these abductions. Now I'm not advocating kidnappers or sex offenders, but it is possible they are getting a bad rap. The big picture here is that a lot of money is being spent to make you believe there are no UFO-alien type extra-terrestrials. Yet this list of unidentified flying objects increases every year. There are many high levels of employees that work for the world leaders, whose only job is to confuse, or sabotage the truth so that people do not really know what to believe in. Satan is the master of confusion. So now you have an array of information and disinformation to sift through to find out what is real. All right then, I have an idea; let's just back up from this crazy kind of thinking, and review a few facts. Maybe it was not a planned terror when Orson Welles scared the world in 1938. And that crashed disc or space ship in Roswell, New Mexico,(you know, the one with four alien bodies found and eyewitnesses confirmed the sighting), maybe that was a huge staged play. Let's forget about the government cover-ups again, and again, and again. And so what if the government is threatening people's lives if they talk or discuss the real truth of what they see, or go through in an abduction? I'm sure the movies during the past sixty-five years dealing with space ships, aliens, close encounters, crop circles, men in black (*the joke*) and always ending with the "War of The Worlds", is probably just the ufoo-grab-the-goo-and-run-fun. But I propose this huge fact that you may have overlooked. In Genesis 3 did God destroy the serpent, (*kill, dead, wipe out, annihilate*) or did He curse him? If the evil serpent who uses mental (*telepathic*) powers of evil is not dead...where is he?

ПOTES

Ronnie McMullen

The Third Chapter

THE MISSION

The word mission needs to be defined before much can be explained. Mission means in Webster's dictionary- task or objective. Another definition is a group of envoys to a foreign country, or a team of specialists or cultural leaders *sent* to a foreign country. So it would be safe to translate this definition as: a group of messengers sent to a foreign country to carry out a task or objective. Most everyone has had a mission given to them at one time or another. Some carry out their task and some fail because the mission was too hard or not planned correctly.

In the late 90's my studies took me to the ministry of deliverance. It is the belief of many that exorcism only comes from a catholic priest. It is a belief of others that there is no such thing as possession, oppression, or anything having to do with demons and the occult. Anyone who has ever been involved with deliverance understands that there are such realities as demons and occult practices. I was involved in deliverance a little over two years and had many people acquire my help. It is my belief that only the Lord Jesus can deliver anyone out of the bondage acquired through occult practices. One of my mentors who helped me understand the depth of the deliverance ministry was a retired San Francisco police officer. I believe the authority he carried in the natural helped him in the supernatural. I think it is also coincidental that I personally trained to be a police officer myself. As a San Francisco police officer, he had many dealings with very bad situations. (Big cities seem to have more crime than rural communities.) In his experiences one of the many arrests he made was a Satanic high priest named Anton LeVay. My thoughts about his story were how creepy or eerie arresting a Satanic person would be, let alone a Satanic high priest! I asked him the question that almost everyone would ask him, "Were you scared?" Much to my surprise he answered, "No." No? I thought. What kind of tough guy was I speaking with? You have to know, this retired police officer was not a muscle-bounder, nor was he one of substantial height or weight. You might say to yourself that this man was just a normal guy. A normal guy, not scared? I began to question him, "What do you mean? How could you not be scared with a guy like that?" Much to my surprise again, he said that he was just a punk with an attitude. Then he began to explain something to me that I would remember the rest of my life. He asked me if I knew about M.I.D.? Oh, M.I.D. Why... Huh? No, I don't have a clue. Then he opened my eyes with- manipulate- to intimidate- to dominate. This is witchcraft. If you manipulate, you can intimidate, which will cause you to dominate. This is the occult's practice of domination and control. Could this be the plan of our government? The controller is the ruler. I never forgot about that information and neither should you.

He went on to tell me about Anton's personal lion. That's right, a real live lion. As Mr. Normal police officer walked into Anton's office, he noticed a very real, very loose, male lion in the corner of this black-walled office. I can only imagine how much fear I would have if it would have been me. Anton smiled and said to the officer, "I see you've noticed my lion." Now remember, M.I.D. Mr. Normal officer felt the intimidation and gave Anton a retort, "Yes, I do see your lion. I also bet that lion cost you a pretty penny. It would be a shame for me to have to put holes into that beautiful cat thinking that it might attack me. You have three minutes to chain that cat up before I make a mess in your office. I have a warrant for your arrest and will be taking you with me as soon as you make your decision." Anton, filled with disgust, chained that cat and then went to jail. M.I.D. is a part of the big picture of fear.

How many times have we been faced with someone willingly or unwillingly using M.I.D. to control us to do or say something in their favor? You might think I am straying away from the mission, but hold on, because I have only scratched the surface. In the deliverance ministry I have learned many, many revelations. Some of these revelations were learned through trial and error. Sometimes it felt like more error than trial. One of the biggest revelations I learned is that everyone is plagued with some kind of oppression, even if it is in the smallest form. Believe it or not it is much like the cartoons you used to watch as a child and the character had a little angel on one shoulder, and had a little devil on the other shoulder. The angel would suggest the right thing to do, and the devil would oppose the angel and redirect the character to another road that would always get the character into trouble. There are not little devils in this world, but there are many demons who have a mission to get you to make the wrong decision, thus putting you on a dead end road! It is not the angel in the movies that direct you to the truth, but the Holy Spirit who is real. The Holy Spirit will lead you into all truth. But what happens when you deny or refuse the Holy Spirit? Isn't that called blasphemy of the Holy Spirit?

Now I want you to be educated on oppression and possession. Oppression is listening and being influenced by demonic spirits trying to destroy, distract, depress, or demonize your mind. Possession comes when you allow or let the demon possess your body for whatever purposes it desires to carry out. Most ministers have no clue how to deal with the supernatural and are stricken with fear. I have also learned the hard way that you must have the authority of the Living God to fight the demonic or you will lose. This also means that the person you are trying to help, (unless you have God given authority), will be worse after you are through than before you started. All because you were not given the proper authority. It is much like making an arrest when you are not the police officer. You were not given the proper authority.

If you notice, I use the word authority often. Jesus' authority is a must to fight demons. So let's keep

> **But truth be known, the demons always had a mission, an objective, and let me say… an order.**

reminding ourselves that demons, aliens and serpents are all the same, yet in different containers. In many of the sessions of deliverance I would speak to the demon. Sometimes the demon wouldn't want to speak, and sometimes the demon would lie. But truth be known, the demons always had a mission, an objective, and let me say... an order. The very interesting findings in my dealings with deliverance were that there was quite a bit of order to this demonic force. It is very much set up like that of our military. I would have to address ranks, orders, and missions, (i.e.: tasks). Certain demons answered to other demons and all answered to one in great authority. In my years of study I never spoke to Satan himself. Also note that Satan cannot be everywhere at one time. Only God can be omnipresent. You will hear people say, "I spoke to Satan himself"... as if they were that important. Satan carries no respect and makes no bones about it. Most people, who have satanic encounters, are speaking to demons... and trust someone who knows, this is no picnic. Out of over one hundred people I have ministered with, all demonic forces I have communicated with had a mission and it was an order given from a higher power. Oddly enough, most demonic forces had the same or similar mission; to destroy or to kill. Demons are not friendly. They can act friendly, but it is only to coerce you to give over your free will. I believe the subject of free will could take up a whole new book. The Lord gave His people free will to make decisions and choices of whom they would serve. He could have made it mandatory to serve Him, but this would have interrupted true love. True love is the driving force behind God and true hate is the driving force behind Satan.

If we back up and look at the big picture, you will find that demons, aliens, and serpents all have the same mind set and are on a mission. Remember me talking about a huge spiritual war? Demons, aliens, and serpents, are given orders or missions to attack every human on this planet. That's right, every human on this planet.

Here is where it gets very hard to understand. I hope you are sitting down. The Lord God allows the attack over all creation. You will even find a similar example in the bible. Now before I start explaining, remember, Jesus allows this attack for our good. Not to punish or mess with our minds, but to strengthen our faith which builds our hearts.

> **True love is the driving force behind God and true hate is the driving force behind Satan.**

Going back to Genesis 6 you will find in verse two that the "*sons of God saw the daughters of men were fair; and they took wives of all which they chose.*" Again reminded that the sons of God were angelic beings that had fallen and chose to be apart from God.

Now if we change gears and go to the book of Job, we find in the first chapter verse 6, "*now there was a day when the sons of God came to present themselves before the Lord, and Satan came also among them. And the Lord said to Satan, 'From where do you come?' Then Satan answered the Lord, and said, ' From going to and fro in the earth, and from walking up and down in it.' And the Lord said to Satan, ' Have you considered my servant Job, that there is none like him in the earth, a blameless and an upright man, one that fears God and shuns evil?'*" It's hard to understand that the Lord would even offer to Satan a righteous man to test. Please note that if our gifts and skills are not tested, we might find that in the day of trouble our gifts and skills could fail us. Remember the old saying, "practice makes perfect"! The Lord that loves us wants us practiced up in our faith so we can stand against the wicked schemes of the enemy, serpent, and alien. As the story of Job intensifies, you will find that Satan and his demons cannot provoke Job. Another notice needs to be taken here. Satan must receive permission from the Lord every time he wants to attack Job. Don't you find this point interesting? If Satan and his demons are all so powerful, why do they have to consult the Lord God first? Why not just do it? You know... Do it? Because they can't. It's called divine order.

Notice also that in the book of Job, when Satan replies to the Lord, he says "*from going to and fro in the earth and walking up and down in it.*" Think about it. Walking to and fro "in" the earth? Is that a type error? Shouldn't it say, to and fro "on" the earth? What about that part that says walking up and down "in" it? Is Satan saying he is walking inside the earth's surface? Did you know there are ancient tunnels dating back to who knows when, that go from city to city under the earth's surface? The more you dig, the more you find. I am going to talk more on tunnels later in the book.

There is an important truth that everyone who believes must remember. This truth is found in Job chapter 2:6, *"And the Lord said to Satan, 'Behold he is in your hand; but save his life.'"* Your death cannot happen without permission from the Lord. The Lord allowed Satan and his serpents to cause major havoc to Job and his family. He allowed Job to go through extreme testing just to see and prove Job's strong and powerful faith. And of course the story ends with extreme blessing to Job based on his love and faith in God.

The question I would be asking is, "What about the people of America? What about the people of this earth? Where is our faith based against the missions of the serpents or aliens under Satan's command?" If we are under attack by the enemy and/or demons/aliens, shouldn't we know how to put our armor on to defend ourselves from the onslaught? But mainstream Christianity does not know spiritual warfare. Most people are not even aware that there is a spiritual war present. We just keep traveling through life, building our self-worth, adding to our growing financial estate or we just struggle to make ends meet. It seems our culture is either rich or poor, and everything in between has been moved to one side or another. The rich

> **But mainstream Christianity does not know spiritual warfare.**

focus on themselves and keeping the investing of money at a high priority. When you have earned the status of wealth, you do not want to lose that lifestyle. And of course the poor have a similar but different focus on life. The poor just try to make money to keep their heads above water, as it seems that they are drowning in a cesspool of inopportune circumstances and very little hope for a successful future. Both categories are so focused that there is little time to see anything spiritual, let alone a spiritual war.

With all of this taking place in our world, in the heavens above, and the earth below, there is a raging war where the forces of good and evil prevail. The Lord God above is calling out to His people and Satan and his demonic aliens are sent with a mission to destroy. You see, if one is destroyed, you can't live in peace with God. Now again I remind you, the Father in heaven has divine control of everything that happens on this earth; good, and bad. But if you are not a warrior for Christ, who are you with? You either wear a black hat or a white one. There is not another cowboy with a gun in his hand wearing a gray hat.

Wait a second! Maybe we can be taught to be gray. You know, not good or bad, just being there. Kind of like the Catholic Purgatory/Limbo thing. Maybe that is where we coined the phrase, "I'm in limbo." I don't want to rain on your parade, but limbo is a state of mind and confusion. It is a state of hesitation and nothingness. It is a state of fear and a lack of responsibility for one's unquestioning belief. Truly, it is a state of death. Dead men walking. How interesting that in the many sightings of aliens, many of them are the color gray.

I believe that we as people are being tested on our belief system. The testing is about the strength of our faith. What can our faith withstand? What pressure can come against one's personal faith without shattering or destroying it? And of course our free will is a huge part of our personal faith. Maybe you will understand the book of Job with more depth and insight. The Lord God allows our personal faith to be tested to see how pure in heart we are.

We may even attend a church, every week, with many people in that congregation. I warn you, make no mistake that those people will be tested on their belief system just as you are tested on yours. And the person who sits next to you in church will not have the same outcome as you will. His or her faith will be individually different than yours. We are each tested one by one for our belief system. Demons are allowed by God to test us to see if our heart is intact with the Father above.

In a later section of this book you will read about alien abductions and firsthand see what I am talking about. Aliens have a problem with God. Demons/aliens have a

> **Demons are allowed by God to test us to see if our heart is intact with the Father above.**

mission given to them by Satan and they don't want a higher authority stepping in and messing up their plans.

Jesus says that He gives us authority to come against the evil one in His Name. In fact, His exact words are found in Luke 10:19, *"Behold, I give you power to tread on serpents and scorpions, and over all the power of the enemy; and nothing shall by any means hurt you."* Now I want to show you some insight to this mysterious scripture. Have you in your travels seen a lot of serpents, you know, Lochness-type serpents to tread on? How about scorpions? Now I know scorpions are found in the desert, but not everyone lives in the desert. Could these serpents be the same serpents or serpent that is mentioned in Genesis 3? And could these scorpions be the same scorpions of Revelation 9:3, *"And there came out of the smoke locusts upon the earth: and to them was given power, as the scorpions of the earth have power."* I will elaborate more, later in the book on scorpions.

There are two sides to this spiritual war. God the Father and Satan the beast. The question is, "Which side are you on?" We think and are taught that there are many religions and many roads to heaven. If you want my opinion, you'll find a lot of roads lead to heaven and when they get real close they have this huge "DEAD END" sign at the end. Then it's too late. Life is then snuffed out and you're in hell. The mission of the enemy is to get you on any road but the divine road of Jesus Christ. Confusion, good works, and false doctrines lead you down a one way street to the pit of hell. Our nation is filled with churches that teach false doctrines every Sunday morning and never even mention a word about hell, a spiritual war, or sacrifice to be with Jesus. Church seems to be focused on getting rich and becoming god in the light of the world. I pray for those false leaders who have been deceived by the father of lies. If one is not

> **There are two sides to this spiritual war. God the Father and Satan the beast. The question is, "Which side are you on?"**

marked by God the Father, they will not be protected by the onslaught of the enemy in the largest spiritual war ever. The seals of Revelation are about to be opened by the angel of the Lord.

One of the most devious missions is to deceive the very elect. In Matthew 24, the very elect, means chosen. God's chosen can be deceived if they are not careful. I have heard the pride of many "wanna-be"

Christians say they will not be deceived. And of course with the pre-tribulation rapture no Christians will go through any testings or trials. That's not what the bible says, that is just what we are taught by our T.V. evangelicals and million-dollar ministries. Let's just get into our first class jets and watch all of the other people suffer because they are not as good as we are. Remember, every huge T.V. minister believes in pre-tribulation rapture. That is, the Lord Jesus is coming back for His people before anything bad happens in the earth. No other country believes in this dung except the United States. Don't you find this interesting? No other country but America believes this baloney. Is there a hidden mission? A hidden agenda behind these false ministers? In the next chapter you might find a revealing.

NOTES

The Fourth Chapter

The Grand Deception

The Grand Deception. Isn't that one of the most thought provoking statements you've ever heard? What does it mean? What does it pertain to? This Grand Deception will center itself right-smack-dab in the United States. The question is... what is the Grand Deception? Who knows about this grand caper? And the question arises regarding this deception that is so large and so magnificent. Is there someone or some group promoting it's inception? Every great event usually has someone or some group promoting its grandeur.

The word grand means: higher in rank or importance. It also means: great in size, magnificent. Now if you look up the

> **I want to remind you, I am no scientist or doctor, just a man of God knowing deep in my soul that something is spiritually wrong.**

meaning of deception, it states the act of deceiving, or the fact or condition of being deceived. In other words, a fraud or a trick.

When I was researching and putting the information together for this book, I came across writings and findings of a term the alien/demons call "The Grand Deception". Men in deep, deep, covert government agencies discovered, in 1983, the plans of the grand deception that consisted of many facets. I want to remind you, I am no scientist, or doctor, just a man of God knowing deep in my soul that something is spiritually wrong. This spiritual war that we are in the midst of is about taking people and dividing them into two groups, heaven and hell, again, no middle. When discovering the plan of the grand deception, there was one facet that caught my eye and quickened to my inner soul. It was the finding of the great rapture. Rapture is defined as: the snatching or taking away. You might have heard this term used in almost every church in America. In mainstream Christianity the "Rapture" refers to the Lord Jesus Christ coming back for His people and taking them up with him to escape the trials and tribulations of this world. One of the most common scriptures used in the American church is 1 Corinthians 15:52, *"In a moment, in the twinkling of an eye, at the last trump: for the trumpet shall sound, and the dead shall be raised incorruptible, and we shall be changed.'* The mainstream church quotes that scripture something like this... *"In the twinkling of an eye we shall be raised up with the Lord and be changed."* One needs to take a gander at the seventh trumpet of Revelation, that is, the last trumpet. Revelation 11:15 reveals the last trumpet. If you travel backwards from Revelation 11:15 you will notice that a lot of bad, bad things

Most evidence is suppressed, eliminated, or made to look like a hoax, so no one will ever believe the truth.

happen. With special attention and warning going to chapter nine. This is the sounding of the fifth trumpet of the Apocalypse. This fifth trumpet is about the world being engaged with aliens, and aliens having power to torment for five months.

Now let's take our viewfinder and focus back on the meaning of the grand deception. What could this mean? I, myself, am going to explain my interpretation of the grand deception and then try to give you some coincidental facts lining up its coming inception. I want to start with fact and truth, so there is no illusion to anyone who reads this book. Most of what information can be found on UFO/Alien realities cannot be proven. Most evidence is suppressed, eliminated, or made to look like a hoax, so no one will ever believe the truth. I'm sure when this book is published I will be made out to be a fool or maybe something worse than that. I don't care. My belief and findings take me to a point to warn the people who have not known of these findings. My biggest find is that Satan and his serpents/aliens/demons are amongst us, and something very sinister may happen in the very near future. Maybe I'm crazy. Maybe I'm just a man who likes a challenge, or just maybe something is coming and we need to pray and be ready before it happens.

Many surface UFO researchers say that the government or the President of the United States is not involved in the UFO phenomenon. I want to quote a statement made by the late President Ronald Reagan that is quite a coincidence knowing the reality of the Grand Deception. This is the statement made by President Reagan at the 42nd General Assembly of the United Nations on September 21, 1987, "I couldn't help but say to him (Gorbachev), just think how easy his task and mind might be in these meetings that we held if suddenly there was a threat to this world from some other species, (alien/demon) from another planet outside in the universe. Well, I don't suppose we can wait for some alien race to come down and threaten us. But I think that between us we can bring about that realization." Now one must ask, why would the President of the United States of America say a wild statement like that? There are probably not a lot of people who even know the President made those comments. Maybe that is "hush-hush" information.

In the 1980's UFOology was at its height in popularity. There was much information being sought about all the unidentified flying objects, cattle mutilations, and missing persons. Talk shows were discussing the unexplainable, and "E.T." was the blockbuster movie. One must keep an eye on Mr. Spielberg's accomplishments. It seems the eighties were possibly an agenda driven time putting our minds at ease about aliens from another planet. The agenda has been to believe those friendly little 3 ½ foot gray beings are here to help us along with our flintstone technology,(at least it was flintstone to the aliens.) We're told how they want to be our friends and interact with us as such. Just tell that to the cattle and humans found in the New Mexico area, mutilated with precise cuts and the unexplainable removal of blood.

Removing of the blood with no vascular collapse. We don't have that kind of technology. No leaks, no trace... Gone! My thoughts are with friends like that who needs enemies?

I'm sure questions are starting to arise and maybe doubt wants to set in. Maybe you feel fear pressing you into a corner to push you into making a choice whether you believe in this phenomenon or not. Trust me, there is no time to fear. Fear will paralyze you, and understanding will free you.

I want to give you a short synopsis of the Grand Deception and the leadings up to it. There are many brave men who have worked in Naval Intelligence, Black Projects, and other deep covert agencies that have come forth to give an account of something very evil, wicked, and sinister going on right beneath our United States soil. Their conscience has awoken them from walking as dead men on the earth. But as one digs to find the real truth, it is horrifying to find out what the United States has done and what secret treaties were signed without the knowledge of the Congress or the Senate. If the accounts, which are told by many are true; I would classify this as extreme treason with intent for a massive second holocaust. Can these stories be proven? Only in the midst of the few that were involved and brave enough to come out and tell about it. Of course we could say and accuse these men of lying and believe that they have a huge case of mental illness to write these findings to post them and publish them for all to see. Again, there is no real evidence. Or is there? Oh what a web they weave.

Fear will paralyze you, and understanding will free you.

The Lord makes a bold statement in His Word, found in Matthew 10:26: *"Fear them not therefore; for there is nothing covered, that shall not be revealed; and hidden, that shall not be known."* It is my belief that something huge is about to happen. Even if these brave men were lying (and I don't think they were) there is something in the Spirit that is terribly wrong. We can just step back and see that our government has been corrupted. It had been my opinion that only recently our government has been corrupt. But I have come to find out through much study, research, and prayer that our United States government has been corrupt for a very long time. And it did not start with Nixon. His actions were brought to light because he was caught.

I am now going to take you down a road that has a lot of bumps, but will save us much time and we will arrive with revelation. You might call this a hypothetical revealing. It starts with a radio broadcast I did years ago. The man's name was Norm Franz. Norm, a Christian author and economist, was being interviewed by yours truly, and our subject was aliens and the Christian belief. Now Norm is someone with a great personality and is most fun to interview. He has done teaching on the biblical perspective of aliens and the church's belief. At the time of our interview I had not discovered the hidden truths behind the UFO phenomenon. I was a rookie in my study, and my mind was boxed to the depth this subject could go. As we were bouncing this enlightening subject back and forth between us, I remember that he mentioned a cluster of UFO groupies who believed that a massive alien rapture was going to happen soon. Alien rapture?!!! I about dropped my teeth! You've got to be kidding, a group of people actually believe that some stupid spaceship is coming to beam them up into space?!!! Talk about falling off the deep end! And of course I asked Norm, "And then what? You know, what happens once they go up into those spaceships? Then what? Is there an alien party? Are they taken to a special place?" I laughed until my side hurt. But what really took me by surprise was the facial expression Norm had. He was serious. I have a great respect for Norm Franz, because he never compromises what he believes, not for a second. I'm sorry to admit it, but I thought he was whacked. I mean, I love this guy, but he fell off the cabbage truck, and he fell hard. Can you imagine, a bunch of UFO'bees standing around in the streets waiting for Dr. Spock or

> **The Illuminati Luciferian world leaders do not carry any regard for the human population.**

E.T. and his father's spaceship to beam them up and carry them off to Never-Never-Land? Ludicrous! It will never happen! Well... I have now come to the conclusion to never say never. Now again, I'm writing a hypothetical theory that's stirring in my spirit and I'm testing it against truthful facts and timely coincidences. When Norm spoke about a false rapture I chuckled with disbelief. What if we opened our minds up and said, "Just suppose." So, just suppose the rumors of the United States signing secret treaties with the aliens/serpents were true. There is a supposed document signed by our secret shadow government (the Bavarian cultist Illuminati), to allow human and cattle abductions for testing and experiments, in exchange for advanced technology including electromagnetic mind control. The Illuminati Luciferian world leaders do not carry any regard for the human population. Just suppose some of these world leaders are posing as popular religious leaders (i.e.: T.V. evangelists and multimillion dollar ministers.) Donations to the church are not exactly lucrative. These world leaders are very wealthy, heavily backed, and carry enormous amounts of power. They have infiltrated every level of government and judicial system. It is my belief that they have also infiltrated our religious seminaries that indoctrinate the schooled leaders to

> **How would you take one third of the population to their death without total anarchy?**

promote their agenda. Now again, we are reminded of the rapture before any trials or tribulation come to pass. This is the doctrine of the NEW church. This is not taught in other countries. This was not taught even one hundred years ago. BUT THIS IS WHAT IS TAUGHT RIGHT NOW!!!

Is it possible that the Grand Deception could be the massive abduction of as many as one third of the earth's population via spaceships? Stay with me. I'm not finished. I have some references to this belief. Our secret shadow government wants our population to be down sized. So if they have made an agreement with the serpent/alien to destroy one third of the population to obtain more world power, then may the chips fall where they fall. Masons are up to their necks in this grand caper. How would you take one third of the population to their death without total anarchy? I know, let's say it was Jesus coming back for His people! Then no one would know what the wicked ones were up to. The most favorite trick that the enemy pulls is being the counterfeit god, or being the imposter of Jesus.

We know in the scriptures that Jesus comes as a bright light. We also know, as fact, that these alien spaceships also produce a bright light.

Imagine if you will, many ships coming together to form ONE GREAT GRANDEUR OF LIGHT, followed by a loud trumpet-like sound, imitating the last trumpet. All at once a third of the population is evacuated, or abducted, or raptured! No one would fear, because they would believe it is their Lord and Savior. And afterwards there are no questions because we know that Jesus just took His people to heaven. Could not this be the Grand Deception?

Why would we have the Masonic T.V. evangelicals out of South Carolina, Oklahoma, California, and so on, guide and direct the people to a false teaching and misconception of the coming of Christ? With so much light from the ships and the extremely inhumane trumpet sound, no one on earth would see anything but light. This would perfectly imitate the Lord's coming. The false teachers have not told the truth about Christ's return as revealed in the Book of Revelation. They have skipped over the details of how Jesus will

> **The people in today's church do not want to suffer at any cost.**

come, and enhanced with great zeal the escape of persecution. The people in today's church do not want to suffer at any cost. This of course is why no study is obtained on how Christ's return will occur. Revelation 19:11 is very explicit: *"And I saw heaven opened, and behold a white horse; and He that sat on him was called Faithful and True, and in righteousness He does judge and make war."* Verse 12, *"His eyes were as a flame of fire, and on His head were many crowns; and He had a name written that no man knew, except He Himself."* Verse 13, *"And He was clothed with a robe dipped in blood: and His name is called the Word of God."* Verse 14, *"And the armies which were in heaven followed Him upon white horses, clothed in fine linen, white and clean."* I guess one of the biggest questions I would ask these false teachers is where are the horses? Hello!!!... I don't see any white horses in their sermons. Where's the army? Something is drastically missing, unless you are not taught what to look for.

A UFOologist by the name of Norio Hayakawa, who headed up the Civilian Intelligence Network, came to an enlightened prediction in 1992.

I believe there is a tie between the Grand Deception and the many false teachings of the Masonic T.V. evangelicals.

He believed that there would be a series of shocking events, timed in succession, starting with a Russian-backed Arab attempt to invade Israel, (I believe it will be American controlled.) After that he predicted simultaneous worldwide earthquakes, a global stock market crash, and a sudden mysterious evacuation of a segment of the planet's population would occur; culminating in a quick "official formation" of a New World Order based in Europe that will last for seven years upon its inception. Norio Hayakawa is no lightweight in the study and research of UFOology. When one acquires forty-five years of findings, you might come to believe that he knows what he is talking about.

I believe there is a tie between the Grand Deception and the many false teachings of the Masonic T.V. evangelicals. This hodge-podge of bizarre understandings starts to make sense when you connect the dots. People with no spiritual background might think that this sudden advance in technology is great at any cost.

Those who rebel against God the Father or Jesus Christ are people who have been hurt or wounded in their hearts. Some of these people have been wounded so long ago that they probably don't even remember getting hurt. The bitterness has taken over and corrupted their spirit. Corruption of the human spirit is exactly what these alien/demons want so they can give their full report to their commander and chief, Satan. And if they give some of their technology to humans... So what!

Do we as humans think they would give up their technological advancements to equal their levels? If so, we might be able to destroy them and thus have no use for their wicked ways and lies. The human race has not learned that these demons are always more advanced than we are. They are a cross between natural and spiritual. We are mortal, meaning in the natural state only. The only way to rid yourself of a demon is to have

Jesus Christ be your deliverer. And not just with words but with true heart. Few in our nation or even around the world carry Jesus Christ as their Savior. In the book of Matthew, the 24th Chapter, you will find Jesus Himself warning the world of the false Christs'. Matthew 24:24 says, *"For their shall arise false Christs' and false prophets, and shall show great signs and wonders; in so much that, if it were possible, they shall deceive the very elect."* Verse 25, *"Behold, I have told you before."* Most people believe that Christ is Jesus' last name. Incorrect. The word Christ means anointed in the Greek. A prophet is one that foretells or is considered a mouthpiece or spokesman for God. Now we can understand the background behind this strong warning. A false Christ would mean a false anointing. A false prophet would mean, one that speaks for God but does not know God. A spokesman parading around like a Godly man, having signs and wonders, yet not being the real article. False, a lie, deceived. Now most of these mega false ministers have something to do with Masons. If you do not know what a Mason is you need to read: Dr. Cathy Burns' book entitled, <u>Mormonism, Masonry, and Godhead</u>. These false ministers have aligned themselves with politicians and have become very powerful. Is it possible that the Masonic evangelicals are paving a way for the Grand Deception, massive abduction?

One of the many questions I have been asked is where are all of these abductees going to be taken? That has always been a personal question I have had. Unfortunately in my research I found where they will possibly be taken. The evidence seems to lead to a remote underground top-secret base located in Dulce, New Mexico and many more underground facilities around the world. Now understand if you do not want to believe, you don't have to. There are those of us that can have the physical evidence put right in front of our eyes and we still would be doubting Thomas'. Doubt is a huge part of the enemy's stronghold. That is because doubt comes against trust. And once someone has been hurt or let down, they mistrust. From that point in their life they doubt most everything that cannot be physically proven. Satan knows that better than anyone. If you think this was easy for me to believe you are mistaken. We can start with the 1947 crash at Roswell, New Mexico. This infamous crash has made world news and yet all of the mysteries of that crash are still not made public today. The United States government to this day still denies that there was any saucer disc crash with alien beings. This is quite interesting being that there were numerous eyewitness accounts including our own United States military. These men and women did not want to go to their deathbed with these huge lingering secrets being held over their heads. They were tired of hearing the famous lie, "you saw nothing, and that's an order!" Civilians at that time had more of a frightening encounter with the top brass of our military. They were told not to speak to anyone about what they had witnessed or else the military, (or the secret handling project for the military), would hunt down the witnesses' families and kill them. This would leave them somewhere in the vast open desert of the state of New Mexico. It is interesting to watch someone change their demeanor in the last minutes of their life. All they believed and worked for just doesn't seem to measure up to where they will be going. What is really wild to watch is how heaven and hell come to a huge reality right before one's death. These witnesses have given affidavits to the authenticity of their encounters. Yet again, the government says that it never happened. Are we to believe the government of the United States of America never lies? It actually seems that most governments cannot tell the truth. Why are the government leaders who we supposedly elect lying to their people and keeping horrendous secrets of treason? Our nation or world cannot fathom this kind of behavior in our government. Thus they come into a state of denial saying that it all must be a lie. Government... Right. People... Wrong. This is the same kind of thinking

> **Why are the government leaders who we supposedly elect lying to their people and keeping horrendous secrets of treason?**

that took place in Auschwitz, Germany when the Jews were led to slaughter. No power over the people could be that wicked. Of course it could be that wicked and evil if your leader was none other than Satan himself!

ПOTES

The Fifth Chapter

SERPENTS, TUNNELS, & EARTHQUAKES...OH MY

If you think you've had trouble up until now, trust me... buckle up! Life is short and there is no time to waste. There are many, many writings of other authors that will go into great detail about the subjects of tunnels and serpents. Just to name a few:

William Branton	***The Dulce Wars***
Commander X	***Mind Stalkers, UFO's and Implants***
Tim Swartz	***Evil Agenda of The Secret Government***
William Cooper	***Death of A Conspiracy Salesman***
Richard Sauder P.h.D.	***Underwater and Underground Bases***

This chapter will deal with a spiritual overview of the reality deep within our earth. Truly, there exists a reality of the unknown deep. There are many that hold to the belief that hell is in the center of our earth. Years ago a story surfaced about a crew that was drilling in Siberia. They drilled eight miles deep into the earth. As the story goes a microphone was lowered and sounds of humans screaming were forever etched in the minds of those that listened. Now of course we can't believe every story that was told, but even so, this one was quite interesting.

Coast to Coast AM radio did an expose on this story and it turned out to be a hoax. But this story turning out to be false did not cause me to stray from the belief that hell is located in the center of our earth. Scripture tells us this theory in Revelation 9:1-2, *"And the fifth angel sounded, and I saw a star fall from heaven to earth: and to him was given the key to the bottomless pit. And he opened the bottomless pit; and there arose a smoke out of the pit, as the smoke of a great furnace; and the sun and the air were darkened by reason of the smoke of the pit."* This scripture basically says that a star fell from heaven to the earth and to him was given the key to the bottomless pit (hell). *He* that is referenced in this scripture did not go somewhere else to open the pit. I believe that the pit is right here in this earth.

I can't help but wonder that the commander and chief of all these alien demons want to give us hints of the terribly wicked atrocities that he is committing. It seems in the evil minds of those that are terrorized by Satanic forces, always want to tell or tattle on what they are doing. Not for good measure, but to cause fear or install terror into those that will accept it. Fear is something you accept or reject. Most of our nation is controlled with fear and generally feel its power and pull through our mass media. Fear *always* comes when we as humans don't understand what we are hearing or seeing. So often we are shocked by what we see or hear. A wall of rejection and/or denial sets in so that we don't feel fear's sting. A natural tendency is to self protect. We need to know that self- protection comes not only in a physical state but in a psychological state as well. We come to a point of rationalization so that we can accept what we do not believe. We do not believe, because if we were to take down our rationalization walls and our self protection walls... We would fear. Most people who have been involved in the UFO phenomenon become mentally heavy and start to suffer from a loss of hope, which produces depression. It does not feel fun to fear and to walk in hopelessness. So denial and disbelief are our best defenses.

Why I believe this stuff is unknown to me. I think the Lord Jesus wants me to know what wickedness is going on so that I can pray, warn, and help bridge those caught on a island of disbelief. Hopefully, I will be used to show people a truly spiritual war and can keep them from going to the pit of hell. The spiritual overview will only put more weight to a heaven and a hell. My passion is for my Savior Jesus, and if that can rub off on you then this book is worth its weight in gold.

Knowing that there is some kind of something other than mankind out there, we must try to understand that these alien beings must reside somewhere... A place to take their abductees, a place to refuel their physical beings, a place to... ?

We are sold a belief that aliens come from other planets. We are told that these fallen angels live far, far away, and come periodically to visit and observe. Again we are sold this, and we buy it at a very high cost, I might add. And of course, we believe it. The reason we believe it, is because if these alien/serpent beings live far, far away, we can "feel" safe. Most people do not want to hear anything else, for if we do, this could injure our sense of "false security". But what if you found out that most of these demonic/alien/serpent beings lived right underneath the earth's surface? What if you were told they had tunnels that lead from one city to the next, just like a massive freeway system; and could move at speeds of up to Mach 2? You probably would not believe me. I don't blame you. I didn't believe it myself until I did the research. Did you know that the United States Air Force has a tunneling machine that can bore five feet per hour? This is based on a 1959 statistic. Imagine how fast they can bore with today's technology. Do most people know about this? I think not! If you are like me, you probably think the United States military is built on the premise of protecting our great nation. Maybe the secrets that are in our government are kept for the good of national security. We would not want the enemy to find out strategic information about our defense systems. (Even though we were sold out by our 42nd President William Clinton.) But I ask you, what would you think if you knew that leaders in our government and the Department of Defense were keeping secrets from the public for the gain of scientific knowledge dealing with genetics and the technology of mind control?

It was only a few years ago that I would have been one of the vast amounts of people led to blindness by the art of self indulgence and high tech "fun toys". Compact discs to DVD's , laptop computers with cameras too small to be seen. There are surveillance cameras to watch what you do...And GPS maps so Big Brother finds you... Maybe I should stay away from poetry.

There are close to two hundred underground military bases and if that was read on Fox News, then the nation's viewers might be overcome with shock. Only a few do the work to know what is real. There is an interesting word that I have found in my research called "disinformation". I like the definition that Webster's gives

One of the most famous disinformation tricks is to go after the one spreading or telling the "real" truth.

for disinformation: false information deliberately and often covertly spread. That's a hoot of a definition! False information deliberately and covertly spread! I changed some words around to give more emphasis. The best way to give disinformation is when you put a little truth into the mix. Because a truth and a lie always equals a lie. One of the most famous disinformation tricks is to go after the one spreading or telling the "real" truth. You know, attack and slander or the "truth teller". The analogy would be... Attack the postman and the mail won't be delivered. Are we not getting a little tired of watching all the government cover-ups, the White House scandals, or the treasonous acts that are perpetrated by some of our most famous national leaders? I'm not sure if we can stop the corruption, but we can warn the people that the corruption is much worse than one thinks.

Now let me gently lead you to some findings that are quite alarming. Out of all the underground bases (huge technological institutions) it seems the U. S. military is not solely in charge. One of the largest underground bases is The Dulce Facility. It is reportedly located underneath the very small town of Dulce, New Mexico. If

The researchers at the Dulce Base have also abducted several people from Dulce's civilian population and implanted devices of various types in their heads and bodies.

you were to travel to the town of Dulce, New Mexico, you would say to yourself, "This is absurd! There is no underground/military/ali en base underneath this God-forsaken town!" You can't call Dulce a "city", because it's not large enough to be qualified as a city having only 2597 in population. While driving in this small suburban town, there is an eerie feeling as you see dwellings that are rundown and lifeless. While visiting this strange little town the one thing that was evident, was that from the few people I encountered, there was no joy or hope found in them. Usually you can look into someone's eyes and see some kind of life, or joy, or hope. Going to Dulce, New Mexico was like visiting a town filled with zombies. The area around Dulce has had a high number of reported animal mutilations. The researchers at the Dulce Base have also abducted several people from Dulce's civilian population and implanted devices of various types in their heads and bodies. (*Note: Livermore Berkeley Labs*).

It is very hard once you start to search for truth. You find out that you have to dig through piles and mountains of lies and deception to discover even one small micro-piece of truth. While writing this book my thoughts would go to: "If I were to read this book, say five years ago... What would my belief be about its content?" I am not sure if I would have believed much that was written. I really think the truth is not that people don't believe, but that people don't want to believe. When you talk about subjects dealing with corruption, a coming end of the world as we know it, or anything that comes against our everyday life, expect to be rejected, humiliated, or flat out hated.

It sometimes feels like people are truly programmed not to believe the truth. And if we move to the religious sector, we find there is flat denial in anything other than the doctrine that they (the select) control you with. It is hard to hold a conversation with someone discussing that there is another world underneath this world that we stand on. A world with evil demonic / alien / serpents who's goal is to wage war with the Lord God Most High. A spiritual war, in a truly natural realm.

> That the people involved with these projects (unless they repent to God), are going to burn in a fire that will be kindled by the anger of the Lord God Himself.

With all these miles of tunnels underneath the ground it is no wonder why we are having earthquakes...Not that I believe that all earthquakes come from the development of the elite building sub-cities and global tunnels all right under our noses. And here's a sub thought I have... That the people involved with these projects (unless they repent to God), are going to burn in a fire that will be kindled by the anger of the Lord God Himself. I do believe these earthquakes are signs by God that something is going on underneath us. There are even bases underneath the ocean. I thought that this was just a rumor. But I must tell you God confirms things when you're looking for the truth. I met this man in St. George, Utah, and we just seemed to hit it off. He began to share about his life, the economy, and then his family. As he kept sharing he began to lean into me so that no one would hear what he was about to say. He told me that his brother was in the military and that he was stationed in Hawaii. He then shared about the secret underground base that was located off the shore of Hawaii, under the surface of the water.

It is so hard to imagine the demented minds of the elite who are trying to establish something so sinister, so wicked, all for the sake of technology. Please understand, it is not my belief that we are being "sold out" just so we can have fun on a new PlayStation.

I once had a man tell me a fact that I would later recall when I least expected it. He said to me, "You Americans have gone too far with your technology. What you think is freedom today will later show it's face as imprisonment." He could see this, as he was from a third world country. I believe we have been sold out by a few elite that have been deceived by Satan and believe that they (the elite) have been made gods themselves. Traced back to their ancestors, they have served themselves, turned from their Maker, and sat their butts on their man-made thrones, and called for the world's people to bow at their feet. Sad, sad little people. They have given their small little minds over to the beast and believed in the king-whopper-lie, that deceived Eve clear back in the beginning. In their minds they have set themselves up as gods. The funny thing is, they have bowed to the beast to become more powerful. They have made covenant with the beast so that they may receive the technology to overthrow him in later times. The perverted thinking of those in power have always sought kingship. And they know they cannot obtain this title out in the open (the light). They manipulate and hide the truth in darkness so that the imitation truth can come forward.

There are many passages in the Bible that we read over so quickly that we do not notice the depth in the passage. The Ten Commandments have been quoted so much that we almost don't pay attention to what is really written in the 20th Chapter of Exodus. Most in mainstream Christianity will believe that I, the author, have completely lost my marbles, or maybe never had them, because I do believe that there are underground tunnels, cities, etc. This statement takes me back to a time when an acquaintance friend of mine used to work in Beverly Hills as a police officer. His credentials were impressive, as he was also involved in the investigation of some pretty prominent figures in Hollywood, and in the White House. He was a Christian with a great personality and a lot of charm. For over three or four years we would visit briefly and have discussions ranging from politics to religion. We did not agree in most of those discussions. I believe that he wanted to believe in the USA as the "top dog", the "big cheese", and that no one can mess with us.

On a cool evening in the month of January 2006, we had a discussion like never before. He is a believer in the Bush Administration and believes Mr. Bush can do no wrong. He is a representation of one third of the general public supporting the Bush Administration in every action of freedom loss in the name of safety. He is one of many who have bought the lie that the government is interested in protecting the people. One of the most intriguing statements my friend made was the proverbial, "If we have to lose some of our freedoms for the gain of National Security and safety, then so be it." One has to wonder if we are headed toward a type of National Security resembling Steven Spielberg's movie "Minority Report". Charge them with the crime before they commit it. Interestingly enough as my friend and I debated the wrongs and rights of our government, he blurted a shocking comment to me out of left field: "So I guess you believe in UFO's. People will do anything for five minutes of fame." He then began to discredit abductions and said that a lot of those people sound and act very credible, but when you begin to investigate these abductions you find out that something is very wrong with them. (If I were taken by a demon/serpent I would be mentally unstable/goofy myself!) I believe my friend was the classic example of "Don't interrupt my paradigm with facts. I want to live in my make believe world." And when you try to pop one's paradigm... Expect to be attacked. I do find it amazing that he brought up the UFO phenomenon twice, never knowing that I was researching and trying to make heads or tails of things. I never brought the subject up.

I totally understand that believing in underground tunnels, and cities, is strange... However there are some legends told about finding tunnels and shafts that lead to so-called lost cities. Many of these stories point to these tunnels and underground cities as being found in the desert of Southern California. I used to ride dirt bike in the desert of Mojave, California City, Barstow, Rand, and Lucerne. I never realized that there could be anything out there but a whole lot of dirt. I did occasionally find mine shafts in the side of mountains with a few boards covering them, but I thought nothing of it. I never explored these shafts because of the many stories of people being trapped and suffocating with no way to get out. Not a way I wanted to die.

I would like to relate to you another interesting story told by a Navajo Indian whose name was Oga-Make. His story appeared in the September 1949 issue of Fate magazine. What we call today the serpent/alien race the Paihute Indians called "ancient people", or "Hav-Musuvs". The article in Fate magazine was entitled, "Tribal Memories of the Flying Saucers". With the Roswell, New Mexico crash of 1947 still not having answers, the scare of Orson Well's broadcast, "War of The Worlds", space ships and open minds were clashing. Many people were just trying to understand and grasp how their world was being intruded upon. Almost sixty years later, there are more people who DO NOT believe in flying discs than people who do. Strangely enough, Oga-Make tells the sobering conversation between an aged chief of the Paihute's and himself. A quote from his story: "You speak in your papers of the flying saucers or mystery ships as something new, and strangely typical of the twentieth century.

How could you but think otherwise? Yet if you had red skin, and were of a blood that had been born and bred of the land for untold thousands of years, you would know this is not true. You would know that your ancestors living in these mountains and upon these prairies for numberless generations, had seen these ships before, and had passed down the story in the legends that are the unwritten history of YOUR people. You do not believe? Well, after all, why should you? But knowing your scornful unbelief, the storytellers of my people have closed their lips in bitterness against the outward flow of this knowledge." Interestingly enough, the old and wise Paihute chief points to a strange place right around dusk, that the white man calls "Death Valley". Now if that doesn't put chills down your back... Then I don't know what will! In the book, <u>Death Valley Men</u>, by Bourke Lee, 1932, there is a chapter that talks about two alleged prospectors looking for gold. The miners named Thomason and White, had stumbled upon a lost city in the Panamint mountains while looking for gold for over twenty years. As the story goes, White relates the bitter truth about offering their find of this lost city worth billions and billions of dollars to the Smithsonian Institution for a mere $5 million dollars. According to Mr. White, the Smithsonian only wanted to give them $1.5 millions dollars. This offer obviously disgusted Mr. White and all negotiations were dropped. According to these two men this ancient city located underground had tunnels, rooms as big as caverns filled with gold spears, gold shields, gold statues, and jewelry. There were mummy-type figures sitting around a polished table that was inlaid with gold and precious stones. One of the most intriguing and mind-boggling statements made by these prospectors was; "They sat there and stood there with all that wealth around them. They are still there. They are all dead! And the gold, all that gold, and all those gems and jewels are all around them." Thomason explained quietly, "These ancient people must have been having a meeting of their rulers in the council chamber, when they were killed very suddenly. We haven't examined them closely because it was the treasure that interested us, but the people all seemed to be perfect mummies."

The accounts of a lost city in the Panamint mountain range and tunnels leading in and out complete with underwater streams and rivers are astounding. In the early days, many men had seen or been in these tunnels. But as time has passed, more controls by state and government have closed most of the accesses for people to find their way into the "unknown". Technology, unbelief, and the loss of tribal leaders from of old had placed a hidden shield over a warning of what was.

I find it interesting that Satan cannot create anything. He can only copy or counterfeit. And if we are to believe that there is a lost city with mounds of gold and jewels galore; it is a mind stretcher to think that Satan has even imitated heaven. When one investigates the stories of old, the mummies that were found in the Mojave Desert in Death Valley were eight feet tall. *EIGHT FEET!!!* To me these would be considered giants.

Giants with spears, and shields and such, sitting and standing around a huge table discussing... What? There's something very spiritual going on there.

Most of the T.V. evangelicals, if truthful, would admit the same thing... It's all about the money!

Even though you may produce light by some source, the underground or undersurface of the earth is naturally dark. In my opinion, Satan is trying to lure people to a false heaven. I mean, if you think about it, why be good, faithful, kind, loving, or patient... When you can be rebellious, hateful, revengeful, and so on... And still receive the gold? Thieves, murderers, and rapists will have no problem with going to this false heaven. In fact, I believe it is possible that the gates of hell could be made of gold and pearl, and anything else needed to counterfeit heaven.

As the two prospectors replied, "It was the treasure we were interested in." Most of the T.V. evangelicals, if truthful, would admit the same thing... It's all about the money! I find this to be an appropriate scripture for the subject at hand, Matthew 6:21, *"For where your treasure is, there will your heart be also."* Verse 22, *"The light of the body is the eye: if therefore your eye be whole, your whole body shall be full of light"* Verse 23, *"But if your eye be evil, your whole body shall be full of darkness. If therefore the light that is in you be darkness, how great is that darkness.''* You see my friends, the enemy doesn't care how he gets you... just so long as he gets you. There are many warnings in the Bible that when taken in the right context, will show you the Way. It is based on your maturity and belief system as to how you can truly interpret the Lord God's warnings. For example in Matthew 10:16, *"be ye therefore wise as serpents and gentle as doves.''* How about in 2 John verse 7: *"For many deceivers are entered into the world, who confess not that Jesus Christ is come in the flesh. This is a deceiver and an antichrist.''* Or again, in Exodus 20:4: *"You shall not make to you any graven image, or any likeness of any thing that is in heaven above, or that is in the earth beneath, or that is in the water beneath.''* These fallen angels have been kicked out of the heavens for their rebellion against God. They are stricken with hatred, rebellion, and revenge. There only solution is to fight the Lord God Most High.

In an interview on the Prophetic Watch radio show dated January 25th 2006, Ex-FBI Stan Deyo gives an account of his belief that these fallen ones have gone underground to use their technology to build weapons and to fight the Lord in Armageddon. What a heaviness and what a

> **Unless we as a people repent and sign on (make covenant), we will face the coming darkness and be swept away into the abyss in an everlasting fire of hell.**

shame to think that while this nation lives in "her" dream world above the surface... below the surface, something evil and sinister is being plotted to wage war against the Lord God Most High. Knowing that the Lord God wins this battle with Jesus Christ as chief and commander is not enough and does not mean you are safe. Unless we as a people repent and sign on (make covenant), we will face the coming darkness and be swept away into the abyss in an everlasting fire of hell. It is not my plan or my desire that anyone would go to such a place. The question is: Are we going to stay primitive in our thinking and continue in our make-believe dream world? These demons/serpents/aliens think we are very primitive. It is to their advantage that we stay primitive. Again, the Bible states, to be *"wise as serpents and gentle as doves"*. This would definitely indicate that these serpents are wise. It would also indicate that these serpents are still alive today. I don't think the Lord would tell us to be as wise as something that doesn't exist.

Remember... we know for an absolute fact that there are many military bases with underground bunkers, and actual building levels underneath the earth's surface: Norad, Cheyenne, and Edwards just to name a few.

Here's another piece of the pie. I had friends in construction that were involved with the building of the Denver International Airport, in Denver, Colorado. These men witnessed some very strange events that took place underneath the airport, as we know it today. In particular there was an electrician who

> **Remember... we know for an absolute fact that there are many military bases with underground bunkers, and actual building levels underneath the earth's surface:**

questioned why there was so much secrecy. He saw men in suits that had shaved heads and looked to be of German origin. He started to get people to open their eyes and question the nature of their work. Soon after these antics, this electrician did not ever show up for work again. Some thought he had gotten sick. What became apparent was that he flat disappeared. There were even rumors that those men of German origin were saluting "Nazi-like" as in the days of Hitler. There are many clues given for those who have their eyes wide open. Murals in D.I.A. indicate Nazism in modern day with a machete's point sticking in the backside of a white dove. This to me is not a form of art, but a form of intimidation to let the public know subconsciously that something is going on right in front of their noses. I think there is an indication of the future stated by Denver Mayor, Wellington B. Webb regarding the Denver International Airport. He says, "Travelers are in for a uniquely Colorado experience when they pass through the Denver International Airport. The works of art that grace the airport create a journey through our state's history and diversity. Like all successful public art, the program at D.I.A. exemplifies an expression of ourselves and provides an opportunity to educate others." Travelers coming into D.I.A. are in for an experience all right! They might need to use their proverbial "barf bags" that they receive on their flights to get through the murals. Everyone entering or exiting from this airport must be subjected to this intimidating visual torture. Welcome to the Mile High City where corruption is king! The mind-twisting events at

> **I always think it is fascinating that the taxpayers have to pay for *things* they don't want to purchase.**

D.I.A. go much deeper than Nazi murals with the hope of burning cities.

If our President is looking for terrorists, he might want to look at the men in power who built and designed this horror house garage for planes. D.I.A. was built in 1995 on a mere 34,000 acres. That's right...34,000 acres, a simple 53 square miles. Why Denver needed a new airport has everyone in that city baffled. Stapleton airport in Denver was ordered closed after D.I.A. was built. D.I.A. was built with less gates and less runways but had much, much more acreage. It is located in the middle of nowhere land. So who knows what could be done there... In secret? And anytime there are secrets, you will find government officials, state leaders and an entourage of do-gooders waiting for a piece of the pie. I always think it is fascinating that the taxpayers have to pay for *things* they don't want to purchase. For instance, a $4.8 billion... Something from another world so-called airport. Yes, I know, it was only supposed to cost $1.7 billion dollars. Could it be that the cost of those huge, huge mistakes that were buried early on in the construction? *You know, the five buildings and the high tech runway.* That's right, five buildings supposedly built in the wrong place, so they just buried them. Hmm. And woops, they built a high tech runway, and put it in the wrong place. Let's just bury that too, with just four inches of dirt. I used to work for a very successful concrete company in Brighton, Colorado. Any time concrete was poured wrong or missed it's measurement, it would be torn out and redone. This company is famous for bridges, streets, and sidewalks. I can't imagine my supervisor coming over to me and saying, " Why don't you jump into that skip loader and bury that bridge. We put it in the wrong place." I also find it strange that the same company I worked for had the bid at D.I.A. for at least one of the runways. A lawsuit is in progress.

There are too many rumors and too many accounts about the Denver International Airport for some of it not to be truth. They moved 110 million cubic yards of dirt around for this facility. That is one third of the dirt that was dug out for the Panama Canal. There are more than 5,300 miles of fiber optic communication cables that stretch longer than the Nile River. Jeppesen Terminal is the name of the main terminal at the airport. It is also known as "the Great Hall". The masons name their meeting place, "the Great Hall". Coincidence? I think not. Something else of great interest is that the entire roof of D.I.A. is made up of fifteen acres of Teflon-coated woven fiberglass. This high-tech material reflects 90% of the sunlight and does *not* conduct heat. This means you can't be seen by radar or that the radar will not pick up heat signatures. And you have to know that I was leading up to the grand daddy of facts... This airport has eight levels that go underground, tunnels that lead to ... ??? Some say Norad. Some say Dulce. Some say nothing. There are low and high frequency sounds underground it has been said, that makes people sick. And to top off this surprise of a cake, how about a capstone with a Masonic symbol on it? On this capstone it mentions the New World Airport Commission. I think this is a *HUGE* hint (*indication, bell ringer*) or such that the masons are a part of the New World Order. New World Airport, Masonic symbols, New World Order. What do you think?

If you live in the Western states you might want to pray about leaving.

If you live in the Western states you might want to pray about leaving. I discovered yesterday that California is 49.9% Federally owned and 52.1% State and Federally owned. Nevada is 87.8% Federally owned and 89.2% Federal and State combined. Arizona is 44.3% Federal and 56.8% combined. Colorado is 38.9% Federal and 43.3% combined. Utah is 67.9% Federal and 75.2% combined. Here's one that's fun: Alaska is 67% Federal and 96.8% combined. Our country has a whopping deficit. Here's a concept... Sell some land!

Alaska is the eye-opening alarm of alarms. Home of the HAARP (High-frequency Active Auroral Research Project) system. This is where the management and control of weather takes place, and also something that CNN or FOX News never report on. HAARP is the birthing of the electro-magnetic fields that manipulate people's minds. Better known as mind control. This was a subject that I heard about in the late 90's. Frankly I can tell you, I didn't believe it. A man by the name of David J. Smith was reporting on former President Ronald Reagan as being involved in mind control. At the time my thoughts were, "You can't control my mind." According to Dr. Nick Begich, author of the book, <u>Angels Don't Play This HAARP</u>, mind control is very real and it is in the hands of the D.O.D. (Department of Defense). It could be used for our benefit, unfortunately since most of government science is highly classified and above top secret, we can almost be assured this technology is not for our benefit, but for our detriment. In a future chapter I will discuss further the warnings of what could come from this top secret governmental science.

I need to add that the underground bases and facilities use electro-magnetics for much of their power sources. Magnetic elevators, antigravity propulsion for discs to fly at an inconceivable speed. So where did the HAARP System get their information? Underground bases and facilities have paved a way for the cities above ground to take credit for what was given underground. These alien/serpent/demons have been trading technology with us for years at the high cost of our human lives, not to mention our innocent children. Minds have been altered, lives have been lost, missing humans just so we can become more wise. Wisdom of the world will only produce pride and take us farther from the knowledge of the Lord.

Pride is to our destruction. 1 Corinthians 1:25 says, *"Because the foolishness of God is wiser than men; and the weakness of God is stronger than*

These alien / serpent / demons have been trading technology with us for years at the high cost of our human lives, not to mention our innocent children.

men." Verse 26, *"For you see your calling, brethren, how that not many wise men after the flesh, not many mighty, not many noble, are called;"* Verse 27, *"But God has chosen the foolish things of the world to confound the wise; and God has chosen the weak things of the world to confound the things which are mighty;"* Verse 28, *"And lowly things of the world, and things which are despised has God chosen, yea, and things which are not, to bring to nothing things that are:"* Verse 29, *"That no flesh should glory in His presence."* You see, this is why Satan and his entourage of demons left God the Father in the first place. Satan wanted the glory, and was intensely jealous of the Father. So Lucifer's Big Plan is to overthrow God in the last war of wars. Maybe Satan thinks that if he sets up his camp under the earth's surface, that the Lord Jesus will not see him. (*Demented minds are hard to follow!*) This is again why I share with you that we are in the middle of a spiritual war. It's much bigger than what *we* think. Let me take you into the next chapter that is sad, confirming, alarming, and might change the way you think about our world. Do you want to be stretched?

�NOTES

Ronnie McMullen

The Sixth Chapter

A Hero Takes A Fall

Everyone today is looking for a hero. Most of the time, since we cannot deal with reality we make up heroes that save our world and worship them as if they were real. We have a man in black wearing a cape, or a man who spins a web and jumps from one building to the next. We have even perverted our minds to think that a hero is one who throws an oblong ball down a field into another man's hand just to score some points for a team. For this we hail them as a hero. Police officers are hardly ever praised as heroes based on the huge amount of corruption within their organizations. This to me is saddening, knowing there are many police officers who risk their lives every day in the line of duty, cleaning up the streets so we as citizens can have a safer place to live. The media is used quite often to get the public to raise their eyes to the new chosen hero. Ron Howard was instrumental with the perception of firefighters in the movie "Back Draft". To portray paramedics the hit T.V. show "Emergency" was produced and aired for years.

I always thought that a hero was someone who laid down their life for another...with no agenda, no glory...just true care, compassion and love for their neighbor. I didn't think that they had to wear a uniform or some elastic tights with bright colors. Yet our nation has an easier time believing in men with capes, than to believe in a Man dying on a cross. The Bible makes an interesting statement about taking up your cross to follow Jesus. This statement did not refer to bench pressing the weight of a cross (although a true cross is quite heavy), it referred to giving of yourself completely, because somewhere down the line it may be you up on the cross being crucified. Few people anymore risk their lives unselfishly for their neighbor. It seems the world has gravitated toward all- out-selfishness.

Every once in a while a hero makes a stand. This hero's name was Phillip Schneider. He was born April 23rd, 1947 at Bethesda Navy Hospital to Oscar and Sally Schneider. Oscar Schneider was a Captain in the United States Navy. He was not a run-of-the-mill, average, Naval Captain. Working in nuclear medicine, he helped design the first nuclear submarines, and was involved in Operation Crossroads. This was an operation that was responsible for nuclear weapons testing in the Pacific at Bikini Island. (*Note: this is also where General Douglas Mac Arthur made his profound statement, "Our next major war will be with aliens."*)

In a lecture videotaped in May 1995, Phil Schneider admitted that his father, Captain Oscar Schneider, had been involved with the famous "Philadelphia Experiment". For many years Phil was very devoted to his government helping them to develop underground bases. He was sold out in his heart that the work he was performing was for the good of our nation. Toward the end of his career Phil figured out that he was not truly working for the government, but for *some thing* or *some power*...that had one thing on their mind...World domination. The term "world domination" is maybe a phrase you might associate with a cartoon or a wild sci-fi flick. But when the unimaginable becomes "reality" it is even a shocking horror to those who know the plan. And Phillip Schneider knew the plan.

Phil had a rhyolitic clearance, which essentially means that he only has to answer to three people. The President of the United States, the head of the Central Intelligence Agency (CIA), or a base commander. This clearance gave him access to almost all top secret information. Common sense tells you, when you know too much, and things go sour, you have to be done away with. Sounds much like the mafia to me, just larger with more teeth. The government, or should I say shadow government, doesn't have a problem telling you their plan, because they will defame, humiliate, and use many resources to disprove you. Lying is always their best defense. But on the other hand, you start putting together meetings and showing people pictures along with physical evidence that the government has sold you out to a demonic race, just so they can enhance their technology, to the cost of children's and adult's lives. They are definitely going to try and kill you. And in Phillip Schneider's case, that's exactly what they did. Cold blooded murder. Unfortunately they had to label and cover up this torturous cold blooded murder... So they called it *suicide*.

On January 17, 1996, Cynthia Drayer, Phillip's ex-wife, received a call that Phil was dead in his apartment and had apparently been dead one week before his body was discovered. Cause of death?...stroke. Maybe the two year lecture tour had stressed him out? I mean, after all, talking about: UFO's, underground bases, the Dulce Wars, the Oklahoma City bombing, railcars for concentration camps, and the fact that the United States has concentration camps (*over 700*), the Philadelphia Experiment (Dad had much proof), and of course the grand daddy of them all missing children... Could these be some of the reasons that Phil had a stroke? Of course, who am I to ask why no coroner ever came out to his apartment after his body was found (*this is against Oregon State law*). Also note that no police investigation ever took even a hint of consideration that items... were missing from his apartment (and I bet you can guess which items.) Their findings could only prove that Phil committed suicide. *"That's Interesting."* There were several attempts made on his life from G-14 Ford vans trying to run him off the road, to FBI agents shooting and wounding him. He was shot in the shoulder two weeks before the 1995 Preparedness Expo where he was a guest speaker. There he showed the attendees the wound from the shooting. Now, of course, I'm no Sherlock Holmes... But it seems to me that if he had wanted to die, why would he dodge all the attempts made on his life? Why not stand there and take the bullets?

The government's protocol is: when they kill you they make it look like a suicide.

Phil developed cancer from being shot by an alien (sounds crazy... But there's more). So, if Phil was suffering so much, and he was, why not take the hit? He was a hero. He wanted to warn the people about all that he knew. The truth is, truth can sound pretty whacked when everyone around you believes the lies that are being told. This did not stop him or make him give up. He could not be discouraged. He didn't gain finances... He lost his life. It seems to me that maybe the investigators could have found a suicide note. There was not one found. The government's protocol is: when they kill you they make it look like a suicide. Phil knew this. He had always told his friends and relatives that if he ever "committed suicide" they would know that he had been murdered.

At the Multnomah County Medical Examiners office in Portland, Oregon, Dr. Gunson determined that Phillip Schneider had committed suicide by wrapping a rubber catheter hose three times around his neck and half knotted it in the front. Questions arose like: why didn't Phil use the 9mm handgun he borrowed from his friend and put it in his mouth and pull the trigger? Painless. Phillip had known the Lord, he did not believe in suicide. This was clearly a message to those who want to tell the truth about the deception that is going on in our government and military.

The Congress and Senate probably have no idea what is going on deep beneath the earth's surface. A very high percentage of those in the United States have no idea what is going on behind the government walls. Deception is growing every day and few people really know or understand what is truly going on. Even as this book is being written, at the exact same time, certain people with destructive mandates are being used to bring this nation down; so the world's leaders and shadow governments can rise to power. What is so mind-boggling is that they are going to do this right in front of the American's eyes.

> **A very high percentage of those in the United States have no idea what is going on behind the government walls.**

I remember going to this cheesy alien museum a couple of years ago in Roswell, New Mexico, and seeing two pictures hanging on the wall, one over the other. On the top, was a picture of a so-called alien spacecraft, disc-shaped ship, and right underneath it hung a picture of a Stealth fighter jet. I never realized how close these two crafts look in appearance. It was phenomenal! Now maybe the disc-shaped craft in the top picture was not alien/serpent at all. Maybe they were breaking in all of us dummies who don't have a clue about what's really going on. Maybe it was an artist's rendition of the Lockheed X-22A Anti-gravity Fighter Disc. Most people have no clue that such a government fighter disc even exists.

Colonel Steve Wilson, USAF (now deceased) stated that "Black" military astronauts trained at a secret aerospace academy and would later operate out of Beale and Vandenberg Air Force bases in California.

Evidence of the existence of the X-22A first came to light during Operation Desert Storm, (this would be under George Bush Senior's command) when American soldiers spotted sightings of disc-shaped crafts in the desert hovering near U.S officers. A Desert Storm soldier stated the following: "In the first day's film footage and especially video cams, in which a large number of GI's had, were impounded so they wouldn't capture any sensitive material."

The X-22A is supposedly housed and stored in a "combat ready", new U.S space warfare headquarters, located in hardened underground facilities beneath the 13,528' King's Peak in the High Vintas Primitive (wilderness) area of the Wasatch Mountains, 80 miles east of Salt Lake City. (I think it is quite a coincidence that when the Israelites were following Moses into the wilderness, that the Bible says this land was called the "Wilderness of Sin".)

Again, remember that Phil was a geologist. In a lecture he spoke about a Stealth fighter, and made a statement of fact that the material used to build the Stealth fighter was made from a mix of materials from the earth and also materials from other

> **...the government of the United States (in a real world of justice) would be charged with rape and punished for the horrific tortures being done to the American people.**

planets. Philip had in his possession some of these material types and would show them to people as he lectured. (*Upon the discovery of his body, in 1996, these artifacts were removed from his possession.*) During one lecture he was giving, Phil stated that in 1954 under the Eisenhower administration, the Federal government decided to circumvent the Constitution and form a treaty with the aliens/serpents. The treaty was called the "1954 Greada Treaty." Officials agreed that for extra-terrestrial technology, "the Grays" could test their implanting techniques on selected citizens. However, the extra-terrestrials had to inform the government just who had been abducted and subjected to implants. Slowly over time, the aliens altered the bargain, abducting and implanting thousands of people without reporting back to the government. The thought that came to my mind after reading this was...rape. I decided to find the literal meaning of the word rape. According to the Webster's dictionary rape means: 1.The crime of having sexual intercourse with a person forcibly and without consent. 2. The plundering (of a city, etc.) as in warfare, to commit rape on, to plunder or destroy.

How interesting to find out that almost every abduction case has something to do with sex. Almost every abducted person has been stripped of their clothing and been probed or sexually examined. If this 1954 Greada Treaty that Phil Schneider was warning about were true, then the government of the United States (in a real world of justice) would be charged with rape and punished for the horrific tortures being done to the American people. Of course this will never happen because the Federal government has no one that they answer to. Complete lawlessness under the guidelines of *their* law. And if they break their own law(s), they just change the law without public consent. Or...do what they do best...LIE !

What a combination! Aliens/serpents who cannot tell the truth and the American government that cannot tell the truth... Now that's scary!

In 1979, Philip was employed by Morrison-Knudsen, Inc. I personally checked out this company to see if it even existed. Much to my surprise, there is a construction company that is very "pro-government" and they have been contracted to build government facilities. Phil was involved in building an addition to the deep underground base at Dulce, New Mexico. The project, at the time, had drilled holes in the desert that were to be linked together with underground tunnels. Phil's job was to go down the holes, check the rock samples, and recommend the explosives to deal with that particular rock. In this process, something happened that would change Philip's life forever.

As the men were working for Morrison-Knudsen, they accidentally opened a large artificial cavern, a secret base for the aliens known as " the Grays." In the panic, sixty-six workers and military personnel were killed. Philip Schneider was one of three people to survive. (The other two men were reported to be in medical institutions in Canada, highly supervised and closely watched as of May 1995.) Phil claimed that scars on his chest were caused by being struck with an alien weapon that would later result in cancer due to the radiation. A man that carries physical evidence and is truly walking evidence that something from another world exists... Must be silenced before the public is informed. What would the public be informed of? Truth. The truth that someone or some elite organization has sold us out to the devil for more knowledge that equals technology.

> ...they accidentally opened a large artificial cavern, a secret base for the aliens known as " the Grays." In the panic, sixty-six workers and military personnel were killed.

The truth is, there is life from another world. It is not a natural world, but a spiritual world. Fallen angels have crossed a line into the natural life. They were kicked out of Heaven when Satan fell. And you might notice that when you are evicted from a place (*especially Heaven*) you might be a bit upset.

In deliverance ministry I have never met up with a demon that was nice. They always had rage, hate, destruction, murder...you get the picture. So these fallen ones will have the same demeanor. Philip knew this because he had a close encounter of a bad kind.

Philip was not a loner. His best friend was Ron Rummel. Phil, Ron, and a few others started a little magazine called The Alien Digest. It started to have some recognition because people always have an appetite for the truth. Phil and Ron went way back. Ron Rummel had no problem talking about how the world's government was evil. In an interview with Ashley O'Toole, Cynthia Drayer (Philip's ex-wife) shared that Ron Rummel had actually worked for a Mr. Lear, of Lear Jet fortunes and had a lot to say about aliens. He and Phil went to the Little Alien Inn near Area 51 in Nevada where they videotaped cattle mutilations. Ron and Phil felt very proud of their magazine. Then the day came when Phil called Cynthia with tears in his voice. His friend Ron had committed suicide in the park. Somehow they knew this was not the truth. Later, Phil would receive a police report proving, without a doubt, that Ron was murdered. Ron was found in a local Portland park with a gun in his hand. He had apparently shoved the gun into his mouth and fired, killing him instantly. Although his hand had blow back blood from the blast, the gun had no blow back blood. This could only mean that the gun had been wiped off after it had been shot. Pretty hard for a dead man to wipe off his own gun! Ron's death certificate still shows that he died of a suicide.

Whoever murdered Ron Rummel probably did not know what repercussion this evil act would have upon Phil. This was fuel to Philip's fire. This was a fire that would not be put out until Philip's own death. He would begin to spread the truth, from place to place, city by city over the next two years. Philip had materials, photographs, and first hand knowledge along with a mathematical brain that would stump people. His father had left him with piles of artifacts that would help to change the public's brainwashed mindsets to the truth about our nation's government and their treasonous ways.

It was in May of 1995 that Phil Schneider stated at one of his lectures, "This government will be overthrown in a time period of six months to two years." How interesting that Phillip's death was exactly ten years ago to the date of this phone call. Coincidence?... Or Warning? The reason the take over did not happen ten years ago was because so many people were warning others and they were trying to get the word out that alien/serpent technology existed. Today we have been conditioned to question if it is even safe to go to the grocery store. We believe in terrorists, not aliens or serpents. We believe in national security, not in the loss of freedom, as in the days of Hitler. We have been re-programmed. Unfortunately we have no Phil Schneider's with us to truly warn the people with physical evidence. The stage is set, the film is loaded, and it's about time to shoot the movie. Is the Archangel Michael getting ready to leave the United States because of her sin and rebellion? Is the Lord God's command to allow America to suffer punishment right around the corner? What do you think?

Phil had a little girl named Marie. Marie has lost her daddy. The hard cold truth is that daddy didn't want to die. The Bible says we are to lay our lives down for our neighbors. In Phil's case he laid his life down for many. A hero took a fall to save people. I know some shepherds today who wouldn't perform this true act of bravery. Phillip Schneider--You are a hero.

ΠΟΤΕS

The Seventh Chapter

"TAKEN" AGAINST YOUR WILL!

We are told in the Christian community that we as people are given a free will by God. Free will to choose which path we want to take. We are told a very similar story by our government. Do you want to be Republican or Democrat? Do you choose to be Liberal, or do you choose not to even vote? Which President do you choose to best carry out integrity and keep our nation protected and safe for the good of all men? Pick and choose what laws you want to abide by. It seems that as more time passes, laws are written to be challenged or broken. We have cities challenging laws, so that same sex marriage is acceptable. How about laws that challenge the nation's privacy, all in the name of National Security? Interestingly enough, the United States does not have terrorist bombs going off in the streets daily, weekly, or even monthly to promote this thieving of privacy. Ten laws written thousands of years ago are being stripped off of our court walls because times have changed. Are we being herded into an age similar to Stephen Spielberg's movie, "Minority Report"? You are charged with a crime before it is ever committed just because those in leadership say that you are going to carry out this unlawful act. When the Lord God gave Moses the ten laws on the Mount, written on stone, this was an incentive to go the right direction. Not to follow this way was really an act of rebellion and self-worship. It was as if they were saying, "My way is better than God's way." The Lord gave Moses these ten laws, warnings, or guidelines to preserve His people from the punishment of depravity. It is my opinion, that the reason the Evangelicals are twisting the truth about free will is because if we believe we can choose whichever path we want to, it puts us as Lord. It also veils a truth that we should fear the Lord. Why would you fear the Lord if subconsciously you believe you are the Lord? This nation of America has lost their fear of the Lord. It is astounding how hidden the truth has become, that we have to dig so deep just to find it. The doctrine taught today is "free will to choose whatever path that is comfortable for you." You may not even agree with this fact and want to show me how many Christians are in America alone. My question to you is, do you really believe they are true Christians? My belief is that they have been reeled in by a hook of prosperity; better known as the "bless-me-club." As people accept this belief that God blesses them with financial gain, the fear of God is removed, and death will be the punishment for their doctrine. False doctrine causes death. Proverbs 21:16 states, *"The man that wanders out of the way of understanding shall remain in the congregation of the dead."* The Ten Commandments were written to give us life. People are taught (by the Joel Osteen's of Christianity) that sin is overlooked, and hell is a figment of our imagination. A real hell just doesn't exist. I am here to help those that have been taught false doctrines.

> **People are taught (by the Joel Osteen's of Christianity) that sin is overlooked, and hell is a figment of our imagination.**

There really is no free will. If you choose a path other than the Lord Jesus, you will have to suffer the consequences of being a slave to Satan. Two roads. Jesus, the Way, the Truth, and the Life, or Satan, the father of lies. Heaven and eternity with Jesus, or Satan and eternity in hell. A literal hell. A hell that correlates with the tunnels of darkness that lead to prisons like Dulce, New Mexico. The most horrific terror I can think of is when you are taken somewhere that you do not want to go. Taken against your will. When someone is forced to go somewhere they don't want to go, many frightening thoughts can enter one's mind. The word, *somewhere* is terrorizing in itself, because when you are taken to an unknown place there is little hope of being rescued. Almost all abductees desperately want to be rescued. When fallen angels posing as angels abduct, they always take you *somewhere*. They always take you against your will and without your consent. They always strip you naked with force and put you on a cold medical-like table. These entities control your mind, leaving you in a zombie-like state so that you follow their command as they lead you through their examination. Isn't this considered *force*? The demonic realm has no problem humiliating a person because that is their nature. Their nature will always be pain and suffering. It would be bad enough for you to be stripped naked in front of humans, and probed with cold metal tools with no compassion for how you feel. Think of the terror in having something you have never seen before do this same act on you for a grueling one to two hours. Not knowing who, what, why, not knowing anything.

About ninety eight percent of abductions have to do with sexual intercourse, sexual probing, studying the reproductive organs, and gathering eggs, sperm and tissue samples. Because *all* humans are taken against their will, their heart rate is extremely high during the first segment of capture. This is why the fallen angels/demons will tell their subject to relax and reassure them that they will not be hurt. I once talked with a very famous doctor who has studied abductees for many, many years. I asked him if these entities lie. He said, "No, they do not lie." I then asked him if his patients had experienced any pain or trauma during abduction. "Oh yes, almost all abductees!" he replied. I asked him in his research if the alien entity ever told the abductees that they (the aliens) would not hurt the abducted. Again, he said, "They always promise they won't hurt the abductees." I said, "Isn't that a lie?" His reply was, "Oh, that's just a little white lie." I would like to know what kind of white lie it would be if it were his pain we were talking about! What they do not tell the abductees is that there is no anesthetic while they surgically cut on you. Many humans have died on their table.

Isn't it interesting that our so-called protective government who signed the 1954 Greada Treaty under Eisenhower, does not seem to care what the poor innocent abductees go through? We are not warned about evil and the darkness taking us against our will. In fact, if someone does step to the plate with courage to warn, he or she is done away with or eliminated. CIA cover-ups have used government propaganda, so that this nation will not find out the real truth why ten warnings are being taken off our courthouse walls, (*the warnings against lawlessness...the warning about where and what happens to you when you think you have the choice.*) The ten warnings are the Ten Commandments. Do not take my word on this. Research and a desire for the truth will put you on the path of righteousness.

Let me show you some grim and sometime graphic findings. You judge. I want to share with you the story of Corina Saebels. Corina was

The Beginning

born in Belgium, Brussels and was a normal every day little girl. Her parents were of the Catholic faith and attended church frequently. Even as a child Corina knew something was wrong in her life. As a little girl, Corina would go to her mommy and daddy and ask them if they would clean the monsters out of her room. Her parents would reply with, "there are no monsters in your room." Of course, Corina would rebuttal her mommy, "I saw something look in my window and it had big eyes that glared at me." And of course to put their daughter at ease they would come back with comforting anecdotes like, "it was probably a cat from the forest sitting on your window sill." Interestingly, Corina's room was on the second floor. Corina, being the sharp little girl that she was again would speak the truth, "Mommy, the kitty had no ears."

Many people who are abducted are not just taken once, but again, and again, and again. For Corina this would be the awful truth. Many abductions would take place in her life. It was always to Corina like a dream state. Sometimes she would just wonder if it was a nightmare. When she woke up in the morning she would have marks on her body. Very unexplainable things would happen. Situations like: her nightie would be on backwards, or maybe her nightie would have strange colored stains on it, sometimes she would wake up and her nightie would be off laying next to her.

When talking with Corina you feel you're talking with someone you've known your whole life. She is sweet, matter of fact, and doesn't have an ounce of deceit in her voice. She has spoken to so many people about her life happenings, including Montel Williams on his show. I believe one of Corina's fears when first talking to her was that she thought I would not believe her story. She admitted that she didn't want me to think she was a whacko. Abductees come to this conclusion very quickly because people who have not been taken against their will do not understand the depth and trauma that abductees go through. It is hard to find people in this world who

> **Imagine something you've never seen rape you, cut you, burn you, and manipulate your mind against your will.**

have any compassion for one another, let alone having compassion for someone who had been through something they don't understand. How can you truly understand an alcoholic when you've never taken a drink? I personally have not been abducted but have been subjected to wild, weird accounts of people who have become prey to Satanic cults. These demons/fallen angels have no compassion, no soul, no love, but do have pure hatred toward everything God has created. I can't imagine a physical manifestation taking me somewhere I don't want to go, and operating on and exploring my body without my consent. Many women are raped by humans. Imagine something you've never seen rape you, cut you, burn you, and manipulate your mind against your will. Most people cannot imagine this. So they don't even try. To top this all off, the government is busy hiding the reality of how dangerous these fallen angels/demons/alien beings are.

When I talked with Corina I wondered how she could have such a good attitude and outlook on life, when her life has truly been invaded. One thing she always relays to me is that when she is taken it feels like a dream state. But how could the marks on her body be explained?!

When her son, Christopher, was just four years old, he had quite an experience. One morning, after Corina woke up from her night's sleep, her son Christopher came into her room filled with excitement and relief. "Mommy, Mommy, you're back!" he exclaimed. Corina assured Christopher that she had not gone anywhere and asked him what he meant. Little Christopher, without hesitation, shared that in the middle of the night he went in to see Mommy, but she was not there. He had gone through the whole house looking for his Mommy and had not found her. He even checked outside to see if she might have been in the backyard. No Mommy. And you might be thinking to yourself... No way! How are these events explained? When one is abducted, there is suffering. When one is abducted, there is a loss of time. Minutes will turn into hours, as these abductees will literally be removed from their place to "wherever" the entity wants to take them. Time is a human measurement. God measures time only for our benefit. Not His. Alien/demon/entities do not measure time because they have no understanding of it. They are part spirit. These supernatural spirits invade time, change time, and eliminate time. When we as humans do not know the right answer, we sometimes fill in the blank with what we think could be the right answer. Always remember, there is only one true answer. It is not multiple-choice here.

> **This whole abduction scenario is completely out of hand due to a bargaining power for technology.**

Corina was missing because she had been taken. When someone is taken from their home they are reported as "missing". *TAKEN* against their will. My question has always been, what do they (the fallen ones) want? They take innocent people up to their ship or probing room, strip them, probe them, and explore the human body. These fallen ones have no morals, no compassion, no love, just a mission. Satan always gives his demons a mission.

I find it funny that our scientists give these fallen ones so much credit for their technology. This whole abduction scenario is completely out of hand due to a bargaining power for technology. It is questionable if the fallen ones would have abducted people without the government's consent. I believe that consent is a part of our will. When our "so-called pathetic leaders" gave their authorization they sold the souls of many people to the fallen ones. God will hold the leaders of the nations accountable, and spiritual leaders, too. Trust me, these people will not get away with what they have done. They will reap what they have sown. So if these fallen ones are so technologically advanced, why must they steal us away from our homes to probe us or use us for their demonic breeding? If our ways here on earth are so pre-historic, and we are technologically in the Stone Age why mess with us?

You see I fully believe these demonic fallen ones need information from our bodies to help them with their evil schemes. I believe that the first thing they want and need is our blood. Jesus says blood is the life force. Take notice of Genesis 4:10, *"and He said, what have you done? The voice of your brother's blood cries to Me from the ground."* Leviticus 17:11, is a key to the fallen ones and why they are so interested in we humans: *"For the life of the flesh is in the blood: and I have given it to you upon the altar to make an atonement for your souls: for it is the blood that makes an atonement for the soul."* The second thing they need is our soul. Again, most abductees who have been killed or murdered have no trace of blood left in them. If you noticed, I used the word murdered on purpose. If you are struck by lightening you are killed. When you are shot by a gun you are murdered. Killed is an accidental death. Murdered is an intentional mandate. How interesting that verse 11 in the 17th chapter of

Leviticus intertwines the blood and the soul. Not by accident, I might add. People may not pay attention to the details in the scriptures, but fallen ones pay close attention to detail in everything they do! Did you notice the wording, that Jesus gave us the blood?! Not the fallen ones. So now you can add theft to the fallen ones rap sheet. The blood is the life. Life for the body, life for the soul. Life of the flesh is in the blood. The fallen ones want our blood, our soul, our seed, and all reproductive organs and body parts. That is why almost every abduction, has something to do with sex. Fallen ones have no sexual gender. God made us male and female. The two become one.

I want to take you back to Corina. She has a description of one of her abductions that might sum up everything I've been saying about the soul. In one of her many abductions, Corina was taken to a huge ship with a huge column in the middle of it. She said that the column had the look of pewter to it and looked as if it were highly polished. She asked the entity in charge (*there is always one that is in charge*), what was inside this pillar? He spoke back to her mind, telepathically, "It is not for you to know". Corina said, "I do want to know and I am going to know." Corina began to walk toward this pillar/column that was set in the middle of the room. She again insisted, "Tell me what is in this pillar!" "You can not know, it is not for you to know", the entity spoke back to her mind. About that time Corina did the unimaginable. She touched the shining pillar and a drawer popped out above Corina's head. She said that she could not see into it because it was way above her field of vision. As the drawer popped out it made a noise as if it were operated by air. The sound was as if air pressure was being released through some kind of hose. As the drawer slid out, Corina began to feel an extreme amount of fear. As the fear overtook her body it began to paralyze her. The alien entity began to speak into her mind, "This is the essence of men." At this point she had no clue what this entity meant by the *essence of men*. Webster's defines essence as: a concentrated substance that keeps the flavor, etc. of that which is extracted; a substance distilled or extracted from another substance and having the special qualities of the original substance. Somehow, I believe essence means the soul of a man. So I looked up the word soul in

Webster's dictionary... And there it was!...the definition of a soul: the immaterial *essence* of an individual life. It also defined the soul as a spiritual or emotional warmth nature of a person; their force. Amazing! There it was staring me in the face! These demonic/alien entities were extracting the souls of men. Not only do they want our reproductive sources, our blood that is the life force, but these very evil entities want our spiritual souls. If you have no soul, you have no purpose. I believe they want to control your mind in every abduction. Only small minded, non-compassionate, evil-scheming demons think this way.

Many of the surface UFOlogists have told me that these 3 ½ -4 foot green-gray aliens are just hybrids, only a glorified robot that is highly and technologically advanced. O.K., let's say they are, who does their programming? There are many different breeds of hybrids. Different shells, same wickedness inside.

Why is it that the smarter we humans become the more we cannot get out of the rain? I have a family member who has one of the highest I.Q.'s and has been to the most top rated colleges, yet he seems dumb as a club to me. He can't even carry a conversation. And *most* of the highly educated individuals I've met are all "me-monsters". It's always about them.

When an individual is trying to help someone, they must know two major factors in order to give abductees help. One, abduction is a spiritual issue. End of story. No questions asked. Two, this is not about you, your fame, your next book, or how much you know. Abductees that have a strong desire for the truth don't give a flip about whether or not you believe them. Guess what, you weren't the one abducted!

> **There it was staring me in the face! These demonic/alien entities were extracting the souls of men.**

Abductees are fascinating to work with. They tell you the way it is. They have experienced a dimension in life that most have not seen, felt, nor heard. You must know there is a difference between abductees and contactees. Abductees, have been taken against their will, and contactees have "seen" and want to "see" more. They are under a huge deception and believe these entities are here for our good. Just wait until they are taken they will change their minds in a hurry. Pain and trauma always make true believers out of people. I believe there is a huge agenda being pushed to open the public's eye that being abducted is the way to receive power and knowledge. Remember again that debate in Genesis 3 over God said, serpent said? Isn't this an exact replica of that? Is this not a repeating of HIStory? If you eat of the tree you shall be as gods knowing good and evil. It is almost as if we as people are being told if you are *TAKEN*, you shall have your eyes opened and become all-knowing, as likening yourself to a god.

Let me give you an example of what I mean. There are many of us that would argue this point and debate that having knowledge is a great and special gift. This is not always true. There is good knowledge from God, and there is evil knowledge from Lucifer. I even believe that there is knowledge that can go either way, depending on who you are.

I remember being around thirteen years of age and being on a paper route with a couple of school buddies. One of my friends was much more developed than I and was like the leader of the three of us. I remember one day in the middle of summer, when I finished my route a little early, my big buddy, we'll call him, "Jay", asked if he could borrow my route bag that I used to deliver papers. I asked him, "Why do you need my bag, I'm finished with my route?" His comeback was, "You just need to trust me." My whole life I've always trusted people, people I don't even know. So naturally I agreed to lend him my canvas route bag. He threw it over his head and we rode our bicycles down to a little mini-mart in town. What was about to happen would change me for the rest of my life. Jay was in the store for quite some time. Finally, after what seemed like eons, Jay came out abruptly and said, "Let's go." My other friend and I were looking around in total confusion, but of course like willing sheep, we followed. We all rode to a huge field with two of us in absolute wonderment. We stopped in the field, hid ourselves behind some bushes, and then came the sentence I would remember the rest of my life. Jay exclaimed with excitement, " Look what I got!" He pulled out a men's Penthouse magazine full of naked and explicit pictures of women doing things I had never imagined. I want to repeat this statement. *I NEVER*

IMAGINED!!! Those images have always been imprinted in my mind's eye ever since that day. Here is my thesis. Did I need to discover this knowledge? Did I need to know that women do these things? My answer is, no. NO! NO! NO! For many years I looked upon women differently, in a way that I never should have. The Lord can get you through any hardship, but it will leave a scar. The same is true for abductees. There is help, but it is still going to leave a scar. I did not know what was in that canvas bag. All I remember was once I tasted of this I wanted to see more. I believe abductees can and do suffer from the same temptations. Once you've tasted of this knowledge, you subconsciously want to know more. But wait, abductees don't choose to be taken, just as I didn't choose to be shown that magazine. I'm curious to know if shame is involved with most abductees. In this childhood event I suffered from shame for years and years.

Almost all abductions deal with sexual situations. The extracting of eggs, the extracting of sperm, and some have intercourse encounters with entities that are somewhat animal or reptile-like. Lizard-like would probably be more precise. Now maybe I've lost some readers at this time... I understand.

I would like to come back to Corina. Again, I want to reiterate Corina's integrity. Many in the field of UFO research who know Corina, have testified to me about her honesty and integrity. I remember speaking with Corina one evening and I don't know why I asked her this question. With great anticipation I asked, "In any of your abduction encounters have you ever seen any form of military personnel?" She answered yes and began to tell me about an abduction which she believed was underground. She even showed me pictures of land in Arizona that reminded her of that time. I then began to dig deeper into the military mayhem. I asked if these men in uniforms carried weapons. Her answer to me was yes. Now let me stop a moment. If this was only in a dream state, then why would these military men have weapons? Are they going to shoot us in our dreams? Or could we say that this abduction was really a movement of a physical body to another place and time? I then asked Corina if these military men looked familiar. In other words, were these our boys? Her answer shocked me! These military men looked to be from another country. She said, "I don't know, it looks like they were from Iraq." "Oh my," I thought, the plot thickens!

Evidence is always required, to believe in the phenomenon of abduction. It is very hard to have solid, irrefutable evidence of one's abduction. This is the same with the belief of God and Satan. No one has seen God face to face. You cannot as a mortal look upon God and live. And no one has seen Satan. Many people have testified about being face to face with Satan himself, yet he does not have the power to be everywhere at once. God does. So here you have: no one has seen God, no one has seen Satan; yet 86 percent of our United States population believe in a God, and a very high percentage of people believe there is a devil. We have the same problem going on with abductions. No one outside of the abductees themselves have seen this occur, yet there are many who believe in abductions. When abductees come forth with their bits and pieces of truth (scars, missing time, ESP, etc.) we give them no credit or backing. We even ridicule them for their odd and often untrusting silence. If you were taken, the tables would turn on your belief system.

A hard truth to believe is that people have been abducted (by an entity), and no one can tell them that it did not happen. The abductees are told, "The scar on your body which has a high level of radiation, was caused by you getting up to go to the bathroom in the middle of the night. Or maybe, there's a microwave in your bathroom and you thought you'd just throw yourself in it to stay warm!" Sometimes I believe doctors get too smart and start to digress in their thinking, because they sure can say the most stupid things.

Let's return to Corina's desert/underground abduction and I'll stretch your minds a little further. In this abduction, she finds herself in the desert. She does not remember how she got there. It is very hot and seems to be in the middle of the afternoon. I asked her if she had ever been to this place in the natural. Her answer was, "No." This answer was given quickly with a strong response. A breeze was blowing and she found herself climbing wooden stairs outside on the desert flats. There were quite a few people with her (forty to fifty), and they were all being herded like cattle, to climb these stairs and step up onto a wooden balcony. As Corina reached the top, she could see other buildings surrounding her that were white. They were older buildings with flat roofs, and yes, they were white. I asked her about the people who were with her. Did she know them? Were they all female? All male? What ages? Most people seem to think that once you become elderly, you're out of the woods... Think again. There are many findings proving that people in their seventies and eighties are still being abducted. As I asked her these questions, she answered me with, "They were just normal people, ages varied, and they were all afraid or zombie looking." Corina said she remembered seeing one lady walking up the stairs that had beautiful red hair. I asked her what else she could remember. "Well," she said, "I remember there were two ships (discs) flying around what seemed to be a compound of some kind. They were flying erratically as if they were dragonflies. There was a tower made of wood, like some kind of air traffic control tower, just much smaller. There was a guard at the bottom of the stairs moving us forward up the stairs. They were definitely moving us somewhere." I asked if the people always cooperated. "Yes," she replied, "It is as if we are zombies." What did the guard look like? She described this military soldier as dark skin, maybe the race was Mexican, maybe Iranian or Iraqi. Their uniforms were tan fatigues with no patches or symbols of any country or origin. One thing she was very clear about was that he was armed with a machine gun. Corina remembers, "That there was one soldier at the bottom of the stairs guiding us up, and one soldier at the top moving us down to what seemed to be a hallway like corridor." I asked her about this hallway corridor. Was it exposed to the elements? Was it enclosed? "No," she replied, "It was covered with a roofline but had no windows, so the wind would blow your hair while walking." She went on to describe this type of hallway and said, "At the end of it were doors." She said there were five or six doors all on the right hand side. Corina then remembered that the guards were telling the people to hurry up.

When she came to the door, her memory stops. This is where she has no recollection. Blanked out... For no one to find out. This happens frequently to abductees. It is like a mind block, so that information is not shared. Unfortunately, most people would not believe this, even if they had total recall. Now this experience, in itself, will not win any evidence awards...but stay tuned! As the world turns.

Remember the red-haired lady? Listen to what happens in Corina's next abduction. She's in the same place, different people, and there is only one ship flying around doing strange acrobats. This time, however, the stairs and balcony are more crowded. All of a sudden, Corina looks up and there is the lady with red hair again. It's the same lady as before! So, Corina calls out to her, "Hey, it's you again!" Oddly enough, the lady with the red hair replies back, "No, you're in my dream again." I asked Corina if she had ever had anything happen like that before? "No," she said, "I don't know why I asked her this, but I felt compelled." What was this lady with the red hair wearing? Corina thought for a second and said, "Pants with a turtle-neck top or sweater." I state this fact that seems insignificant right now, because we will come back to the turtleneck.

Again we ask... Where's the evidence? Now we can get to the "Oh my God!" stuff.

Because Corina is a bold and courageous woman, she is not going to be silent or passive with what has happened to her. She has been on many radio programs and some T.V. programs as well. While listening to a radio broadcast, the woman with the red hair (we'll name her "Dakota" for privacy issues) heard Corina telling her story. Dakota's intrigue with Corina was overwhelming. She felt she just had to get a hold of Corina and talk to her for some reason. This feeling was lodged deep inside her heart. So she called the radio station and asked if somehow she could talk to Corina. The secretary took her name and said she'd give her number to Corina and told her, "If she chooses, then she will call you." Dakota hung up the phone with hope. A little later, after the show was aired, Corina phoned Dakota and they seemed to share some strange bond that neither of them could explain. From that time forward Corina and Dakota had become very close friends. You might say, they were long lost sisters. They were so glad they had been brought together as friends, even if it was in an unusual way.

One day when Corina was on the phone with Dakota they mentioned that they needed to get together some time in the near future. Neither one had ever seen the other. They were curious how they would look. Corina suggested that they exchange photographs until they could meet. They both agreed and soon received a letter from one another in the mail. How exciting it would be to finally see a picture of what her friend looked like after only hearing her voice by phone after all this time. As she gazed at the photo of Dakota, a strong emotion, almost to the point of disbelief entered. You see, Corina was not prepared for the effect it would have on her. Dakota WAS the woman with red hair wearing the turtleneck top! This was the same woman she had seen in her abductions. Twice Corina had seen Dakota in her dream state, and now, right before her eyes, she held a picture of the woman who was abducted and taken to the same place. Coincidence? No, this was now hard evidence. Now of course, there are always those who could be sitting on a horse and if you told them that they were sitting there, they still would not believe you. Unfortunate... But true!

Now they knew why their close-knit relationship felt so strong. As they discovered their common ground, they were able to cry together, share with one another, and trust each other. Abductees have a hard time with trusting because they had been so violated. They might trust someone who carries understanding and compassion (these are rare to come by). One day, while Corina and Dakota were sharing the subject came up about their childhood and upbringing. Dakota began to share about a time she remembered when her parents drove her out to a farm. There was a group of adults and children. The adults went inside, and were acting like zombies. She said it was kind of weird. She began to go on with her story of the farmhouse, how she was sitting on the front porch with her legs dangling over the edge, watching some children play in the yard. There was a girl that stuck out in her memory, holding hands with the other children and skipping in a circle... Then they stopped. Before Dakota could go on with her story, Corina interrupted her and said, "I'm not trying to be rude, but do you remember what you were wearing that day?" Dakota said, "Yes, I do. I was wearing..." "No!" retorted Corina, "Let me tell you what you were wearing and see if I'm right." "O.K.", Dakota replied with quiet anticipation in her voice. Corina then began, "You were on this porch in front of an old farmhouse and then sat down with your legs hanging over the edge. You were barefoot. Your top was white with short sleeves. You were wearing a red and navy plaid skirt, and you were about five or six years old." Corina could hear the emotion rising in Dakota's voice. "How could you know that?!! That was exactly what I was wearing! I remember, I remember..." exclaimed Dakota in tears. "How could you know what I was wearing Corina?!" After a few seconds of silence, Corina said quietly, "I was the girl holding the children's hands and skipping around. That was me, I remember the farmhouse. I remember you on the porch. I remember your bare feet. I remember ALL of it!" They began to cry with each other combined with a bag of mixed emotions. Joy, surprise, relief, and many other emotions played in their hearts through this view into their past. They were not crazy, it was now confirmed. They both had been taken against their will since childhood.

How many more have been taken in the same way? How many have tried to share their experiences and have been ridiculed? How many have not remembered their experiences? How many remember, yet have not mustered enough courage to share their experiences? Is it possible the ridicule is set up as a propaganda, initiated from various media's who have signed on to give disinformation and muddy all clear waters "in the name of the New World Order"? The word to remember is ... The truth shall set you free. If Big Brother has a covenant with these fallen ones, maybe it's important that they mock those who have true experiences. Is it possible that Big Brother has hired those to corrupt the truth, silence those that carry it, and install fear to those who would want to find it?

Corina and Dakota are only two of those who populate this vast wide-open planet that we call earth. How many millions and billions of people on this earth have had similar experiences and need to share them? The truth shall prevail if we act accordingly. We must fight the good fight. We must stand for our brothers and sisters, not tear them down. People, abduction IS real! There is a vast amount of people taken against their will every day. There is governmental genetic engineering taking place underground and above the earth every day. Do we just sit on our royal duffs and do nothing while the enemy (Big Brother, fallen ones, etc.) drives his huge semi truck of tricks and schemes to eliminate this people? What happened to the God-fearing people? What happened to standing up (confronting) for what's right? Some people just don't know. They truly are naïve. But let me shed some light on a dark subject, they will soon come "into the know." Like it or not, they will come "into the know!" Wait and see.

Ronnie McMullen

∏OTES

The Eighth Chapter

Coming Into The Know

Sometimes the truth can be grueling to find. Through the many overwhelming hours of research, drudging through piles of papers, sorting out what is true, and discovering who is pushing an agenda, one has to find and place the missing pieces of the true puzzle together. Many researchers start with a heart to help and warn people of this bleak, but true phenomenon. However, as time passes, fame and pride distort the original reasons why the researcher began his or her study. Fame and

> Some government leaders carry a worse record than those who inhabit the prisons.

fortune are the destroyers of many, which have blocked the truth from getting into the hands of those who need it. I once had someone very wise tell me, "Truth is almost becoming illegal to tell."

Our judicial systems have become so corrupt that all you have to do is know someone, have some money to pay them, and you can get away with anything. The children of today are doomed by a loss of hope because of our government leaders and the choices they've made. Some government leaders carry a worse record than those who inhabit the prisons. Can you imagine working for a company that has a little more than 500 employees and has the following statistics:

29 accused of spousal abuse
7 arrested for fraud
19 writing bad checks

117 bankrupted at least two businesses
3 arrested for assault
71 cannot get a credit card due to bad credit
14 arrested on drug-related charges
8 arrested for shoplifting (theft)
21 current defendants in lawsuits
84 stopped for drunk driving in 1998 alone
217 stopped for offenses ranging from speeding to DUI in 1999

And by the way, these statistics happen to be from our 535 members of Congress. Also in 1998 and 1999, these members claimed Congressional immunity and were not prosecuted. What does this have to do with the tea in China you say!? If these statistics serve correctly, then we are safe to say that 69% of our Congress in 1998 were corrupt in some fashion. This is just a percentage of who was caught. Is the Senate just as dirty? There are a few in high places that have shared with me that something deep and dark is birthing in our government. What is all of this corruption tied to? Remember, there is black... And there is white. Maybe gray is classified as not getting caught? If these stats are to be less than true, we are in grave danger. How can so-called elected officials not stand for what is right while serving their country? This is only a pinhole of what is seen by the public.

What if we were to shine a spotlight on what is not seen? In other words, what if we were to expose the truth of the alien agenda and of the New World Order with their perverted thoughts and ideas on alien abductions?

> **How can so-called elected officials not stand for what is right while serving their country?**

Many researchers are busy trying to prove that these entities are real without any compassion for what the victim has gone through. Their entire focus is to prove that aliens are real and to show the public their latest findings. Here are my simple thoughts: "Who gives a flying flip on the latest findings?" We should be helping the ones who are being victimized by the fallen ones and presenting solutions rather than evidence. Many only want to use the victims to promote their fame and prosperity. I urge you as a reader to try with everything in you to understand that this is a spiritual war. If you are on the wrong side of the spiritual fence, you could be the next victim. Maybe you are already a victim and have not come "into the know." What do I mean? Let me explain. Much to my surprise, I found out that many abductees do not realize that they have even been abducted until they reach between the ages of 30 and 35. I'm not saying that the abductions started at 30-35 years old, but this seems to be the magical number when people come "into the know." They know that something has happened to them and they know it has been happening for quite some time. Up until now, they were hiding in denial. Maybe this age of 30-something is when our minds are strong enough to take the emotional stress that we have been taken against our will since childhood for someone else's

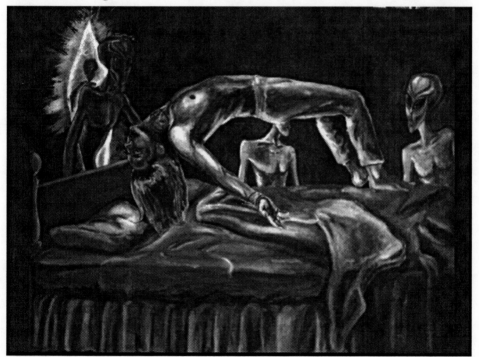

technological advances. I believe these entities are not as advanced as they want us to believe. I might add that if you are not searching into the spiritual arena, there will be much data that you might be missing. Some of these researchers will be filled with data and evidence that will not guide them to a solution.

We must understand that we are dealing with spiritual beings that have experienced things that we have not. These entities have transcended time and dimensions that we as humans do not understand. If you are trying to help those who have been victimized by these fallen angelic entities, and you are not in the spiritual "knowing", then you are in the natural "knowing". This means that the door is shut to you because spiritual and natural realms are so completely different.

These fallen ones operate in the spiritual realm first, and then the natural. There is always an order to their mission. There is an order and a command given by the one highest in authority. Always! Natural methods do not work on these entities. We here on earth, do not have the technology or the methods to overthrow these beings. Many entities allow people to be fooled by playing along with whatever physical evidence that humans have been allowed to discover.

The spiritual realm is much like fog. In the spiritual realm, your vision opens up into another dimension. Most who are abducted cannot tell you how they were transported from here to there, or from there to here. It just is. But if you press further into the abduction scenario you will find that their memory recalls many sights, sounds, and smells. Yes, smells. Dreams don't usually smell... But encounters do. Why? Because they are real.

Why don't people share their experiences before their thirties? I believe it is possible for people to remember their encounters before then. It is my theory that when these events surface in their memories, they first try to release this information to their loved ones. This usually doesn't help, because when you speak of something that has happened to you, and it doesn't fit into someone else's proverbial *box*; they reject your cry for help and will probably reject you as well. You are then labeled as weird, wacko, or one who will go to any extreme for attention, etc. Who wants all of this dung flung on them? The solution to this scenario is to stay quiet, don't share, shut up, etc. After you have been rejected by those you love and trust, why tell anyone else?

Why are more females coming forward than males? I believe that more women are abducted than men, mostly for their eggs, but also because of their demeanor. I believe it is possible that women can handle it emotionally better than men. And of course, our government leaders have helped those who have doubt and fear to become more pronounced in those beliefs. All of this works against the abductees.

Also, churches are the worst place to receive help. Many people have shied away from the modern mainstream church because of their hypocrisy, greed and because they are judgmental. Why would an abducted person want to find shelter in a place where fear, doubt, and judgment rule? The abductees that I have spoken with, have tried to seek help from the church all to find out the solemn truth...that most preachers cast judgment upon them. Some preachers have gone as far as to state that devils and demons have played with the abductees and they accused them of it being all of their fault. This is the place where this author explodes! How can it be the child's fault when their abductions started at such a young age? If a robber comes to rob the bank while you're making a deposit, is it your fault you were in the bank at that time? That's ludicrous thinking! The only ones with that kind of thinking would be... Our government?

While at the 2006 UFO Interactive Conference in Denver, Colorado, I was given the opportunity to meet a veteran UFO researcher. His name is Graham Conway from Canada, director of UFO B.C. Graham has been studying this phenomenon for over 60 years. One could obtain much information just spending a mere hour with him. He began to share with me some of the questions that he asks people who believe they have possibly been abducted. But, before I share with you these simple yet profound questions, I want to give you some food for thought. Right now it might be crossing your mind, or somewhere lingering in your subconscious, the thought: "Could I possibly have been abducted?"

Let me share with you some startling information. While I was at the 2006 UFO Interactive Conference, I was able to huddle together some of the guest speakers including: Graham Conway, UFO B.C.

Stan Deyo, spacecraft engineer who worked with Dr. Edward Teller.

Corina Saebels, abducted since the age of five.

I recorded them all together on one interview for my radio program, and asked them some pretty "in-your-face" questions. The guests interacted with each other and shared their experiences. In the back of my mind, I had something that I wanted to be validated as true. In my research I had come across a man who stated that "one in ten" people are chipped with a tracking device or other mechanism that is inserted through the nasal cavity and up into their brain. This device allows the fallen ones to track and monitor their subjects on a full time basis. As I went around the table and asked each guest if they believed this fact to be true, every one of them did not hesitate to more than agree and answer, "Yes!" I was amazed! Actually I was shocked! In fact, their thoughts were, "More than one in ten." I had to close my mouth at this time for fear of looking like a moron. They did not say, "Yes I heard that fact from so and so...", it came from their own experiences and research. As I shared earlier, the man who stated the "one in ten" figure said that this was based on facts from years ago. Today, it could be as high as one in seven. I know you're struggling with this alarming figure. Just hang on a second as we continue down this road of mystery. I believe this explains the nose bleeds and headaches these victims suffer from. I call these people victims because they did not ask for this. They did not sign up for this course, *"Let me be your guinea pig so you can develop your own race."* No! They were sold out by leaders who should never have been in power. People were exchanged for technology. The scary tale is that this technology changes the human race into their desired race, the Nephilim.

If people (*victims*) don't remember their experiences, or if they remember but do not want to share them for fear of being ridiculed, how will we ever truly know how many there are? The governments around the world are not going to open up their classified documents. They're not going to let the general public mosey on into their offices to comb through their *secret* files on abductions, and share the travesties of possibly millions. It is the secret that will not be exposed... Until it is too late! Those who disbelieve will be shocked and overcome with fear and terror, to the point of their hearts failing them. Of course there will be those who stand "in the know" and say, "I told you I'm not crazy! See, I told you so!"

You might want to stop and pray or meditate before reading these questions. They could bring you into the "know". Now... The questions:

1. Do you believe you have been abducted?

2. Have you had visitations or think that you have been visited by something unexplainable?

3. What happened to you as a child? What did your parents think about your experiences?

4. Have you ever had lights come into your room, golf-ball-like, intelligently controlled, searching for something?

5. Have you ever had a clicking, humming, beeping, chirping, whistle in your ear type of noise?

6. Have you ever woken up with marks on your body, behind your ears, or a lump on your neck or head?

7. Do you move a lot? Do you feel like you are running from someone or something?

8. Do you have nosebleeds? How often?

9. Do you have headaches? How intense? Are your eyes sore? Do you have a metallic taste in your mouth? Do you have a bad smell on your skin that is hard to wash off?

10. These people that visit you, why do you refer to them as light people? Are they friendly?

11. When these lights visit you, do you suffer from paralysis? Are you able to freely move? Do you feel you are in control during these visitations?

12. Do you feel that when you are taken, you are somehow fed information? Does it feel like school? Are you able to understand all that you are receiving?

13. Do you ever find yourself waking up in unusual places? Do you ever wake up with dirty feet, grass in your bed, or footprints on the floor?

14. When you go to bed in whatever you're wearing, do you find that the next morning your P.J.'s or nightie is on inside out? Are you wearing it backwards? Or when you wake up are you naked with your clothes lying next to you?

15. How long have you been sleepwalking? Do you sleepwalk in a house with an alarm system, but yet for some strange reason you don't set it off?

16. Are you afraid of certain roads or places? Are you afraid of what happens on those certain roads or places?

17. Have you ever woken up and something around you or in your room was damaged in a strange manner?

18. How are you taken out of your room or place of dwelling? Are you levitated? How do you exit?

19. Have you been aboard anything or seen the inside of what you believe to be a craft? What is it that you see? Is their technology different than ours?

20. When you are taken, what happens to the temperature? Does it change?

21. Do you ever see anyone you know when these events take place?

22. Do you have pets? Do they react when these events take place? Is their behavior unusual during these occasions?

23. Since these events, have you become more psychic in your abilities to understand what the future holds? Are you more artistic?

24. Have your parents ever mentioned events, similar or exactly the same, happening to them?

25. What is your ethnic background? Are you Jewish or Native American?

26. Do you find this phenomenon to be in your parents? Do you see strange events happening to your children? Have you talked about these occasions with your brother or sister?

27. Does this usually happen at night or in the day? Have you suffered from a loss of time, not knowing where or what you have been doing for one to three hours?

28. Are you a man or woman of faith? Does your faith involve Jesus Christ as Lord and Savior? Have you ever spoken to these light people about Jesus Christ? What is their reaction?

29. Do they communicate to you differently than speaking? Do they communicate to you that they won't hurt you? Do they hurt or harm you in anyway? Do you feel violated?

30. And last, do not think about or ponder thoughts after you read this next phrase, Just respond. "It is time".

These are just surface questions that go much deeper. There are more facets to the depth of how they are asked and how the individual replies. Many in UFO research have forgotten about compassion for those who have been victimized by these disturbing events. There are those people who like to try and deceive the UFOlogists into believing they have been abducted and taken into some spaceship to a far away galaxy. Those that find this humorous will receive their just reward. Anyone who truly chases after the truth in UFO research will spot the counterfeit. There is always a counterfeit. The counterfeit is placed as a distraction so we cannot find the original.

If you have read these last few pages and your heart rate has increased, or if you are suffering from fear or anxiety, I want to comfort you with these words: "It will be all right! Help is coming if you allow the truth to save you." The truth is the only comfort one can receive in these situations.

In the last chapter of my book I will present what I believe to be the defense suit against these entities that take us against our will. They come as a *"thief in the night"* stalking our women, our children, and yes, even our men. They come and violate our rights as human beings and leave us helpless with their mind control. They

> **The human race is being altered so that everyone comes under domination.**

manipulate, to intimidate, to dominate. They are not our friends. They have come to distract us with their technology and to deceive those in government leadership who allow their presence. They will seek, steal, and destroy, with or without consent.

History is repeating itself as you are reading the words on these pages. Genesis 6 is regurgitating right in our midst. The human race is being altered so that everyone comes under domination. The Nephilim are here! Do you doubt? Just wait until the next chapter. You might find giants hiding in places and changing their form to fit in undetected. Are you coming "into the know?" Only you can make that decision.

ᑎOTES

Ronnie McMullen

The Ninth Chapter

PRACTICE MAKES PERFECT THE NEPHILIM ARE HERE!

What a startling title to begin a chapter with! The Nephilim are here! Says who? How do we know? And ... what is a Nephilim, again? If these are some of your questions, let's go back to Genesis 6:1-5 " *And it came to pass, when men began to multiply on the face of the earth, and daughters were born to them, That the sons of God saw the daughters of men that they were fair; and they took them wives of all which they chose. And the LORD said, My Spirit shall not always strive with man, for that he also is flesh: yet his days shall be a hundred and twenty years. There were giants in the earth in those days; and also after that, when the sons of God came in to the daughters of men, and they bore children to them, the same became mighty men which were of old, men of renown. And God saw that the wickedness was great in the earth, and that every imagination of the thoughts of his heart was only continually evil all the time.*"

There are some startling finds in these first five verses of Genesis. First, we discover the sons of God, better known as the fallen angels, finding the daughters of men fair, beautiful, and taking them for wives. Many pastors and religious leaders have been confused on the phrase "sons of God". They believe the sons of God to be humans.

You will find in the Book of Job 1:6, "*Now there was a day when the sons of God came to present themselves before the Lord, and Satan came also among them.*" Are we to believe these are ordinary men presenting themselves before the Lord along with Satan? *Sons* come from the Hebrew word *ben* or *bane*, meaning a son in the widest sense. It can also mean afflicted, anointed, appointed, etc. You will also find in its definition: rebel, robber, x servant born, x soldier, son. I believe this would mean fallen one. The word *God* in this Hebrew translation means Elohim (El-o-heem), meaning Supreme God. These sons of God are the angels of the Supreme God who have fallen from the throne, and are now cast down upon this earth. So ... if they (the fallen ones) were cast from the heavens above, because their focus and understanding of the Supreme God has changed...Is it possible that their demeanor could change too? Maybe now it is one of corruption and revenge? Remember, fallen ones have spiritual power. Make sure you understand that these fallen angels are not ghosts. They can manifest in a physical body when needed.

Let's dissect Genesis 6:4, *"There were giants in those days; and also after that."* What does that statement mean? *"And also after that."* Remember, this is the timing of the great flood. Christian theology points to everyone being destroyed by the flood except for Noah and his descendants, but that seems to contradict Genesis 6:4. I'll take God's word over man's word any day!

Were these fallen ones up to no good? Of course, what were these fallen ones up to? Genetic engineering. They wanted to corrupt the genetic line of man so Jesus could not be born pure. The Bible says there were giants in those days, not large men ...but giants! They weren't just corrupting men. They were corrupting the vegetation as well. In the Bible (Numbers Chapter 13), there were twelve spies sent into the land of Canaan. They were to come back and report to Moses what they found. One man from every tribe (twelve in all) was selected to go and assess the

> **Can you imagine cutting one cluster of grapes and carrying it on a pole between *two* men?**

land ... To observe the people in the land, to see if they were strong or weak, few or many ...to see if the land was good or bad, fat or lean. These twelve sent were commanded to bring back the fruit of the land. It says in the Bible that this was the time of the first ripe grapes. Numbers 13:23 says, *"And they came to the brook of Eshcol, and cut down from there a branch with one cluster of grapes and they bore it between TWO upon a staff; and they brought of the pomegranates and of the figs."* Reading this verse for the first time can be a shocker. Religious leaders or those who only read the surface really struggle with this one. After forty days they returned to Moses with a report. Can you imagine cutting one cluster of grapes and carrying it on a pole between *two* men? Those had to be softball size grapes! As these twelve spies returned, they began to share their fears of going into this land of milk and honey. Why, because this land was filled with giants. Look at Numbers 13:32-33, *"And they brought up an evil report of the land which they had searched to the children of Israel, saying, the land, through which we have gone to search it is a land that eats up the inhabitants thereof; and all the people that we saw in it are men of great stature. And there we saw the giants, the sons of Anak, which come of the giants: and we were in our own sight as grasshoppers, and so we were in their sight."* Only Caleb and Joshua stood up out of the twelve and said, *"Let us go up at once and occupy it; for we are able to overcome it."* This confirms Genesis 6:4, *"There were giants in those days, and also after that."*

Remember King David? What did he fight? A giant. These giants of old ranged in height from eight to thirteen feet tall. Some are larger than that. If the Nephilim are here, how come we don't see them? They should stand out like spilt catsup on a white shirt. But they don't. Let me tell you why. Practice makes perfect...genetic engineering.

Months ago I interviewed Dr. David Jacobs, UFOlogist. In some of his sessions of hypnotism, the fallen ones would show the abductees pictures of people that resembled their own family portraits. These entities would ask, "Do you see any difference between us and you?" The abductees would answer, "No." These entities would come back with, "You see, we are just like you. There is no difference." They have been practicing for quite some time.

Man wants to take credit for the huge increase of technology that has advanced us so rapidly, even in these last ten years. Man's pride is always a problem. We always boast about our science, our thought process, our creativity, and of course, our belief. But have we received help from another source? I know God has given man many gifts, but with the gain of too much knowledge, comes consequences. Right or wrong, integrity or corruption, pride or humility ... The world has a very narrow view of what is really going on. Our technology has far surpassed what most people would ever imagine. Our secret world leaders have been up to no good for quite some time now. Their research has been self-serving, immoral, without consent, and very deliberate. Our world leaders have partnered with the fallen ones to learn a deeper technology in order that they might gain more control over this earth. These leaders have corrupt minds. There is a cost for having an alliance with Satan and his fallen ones. These mortal men cannot come against the wicked schemes of Lucifer. They think they are equal with Satan... Get a clue, Satan does not share his power! This is all part of the great delusion, or should I say, The Grand Deception. Lucifer, the father of lies, is going to lead this nation straight to hell itself if he can.

I think as you begin to read the words ahead, you might struggle with disbelief, but let me inform you, I completely understand. I would struggle as well, but first hand knowledge plays no favorites. I want to tell you the story about Angel and Billy. I have changed their names due to the sensitivity of this story. Picture this as the old television series "Dragnet" ... the names and places were changed to protect the innocent. Angel was a beautiful woman looking for family and love. She was a woman who found pleasure in giving rather than receiving. She had an understanding of God and spent her time enjoying life. Unfortunately, sometimes life deals unfairly. Angel had been taken from a very early age. She only knew a life of being preyed upon, yet still made the best out of what life dealt her. Angel was not a complainer. It is important to know that Angel was chosen by these fallen ones/demons for whatever reason. The fallen ones/demons can do nothing in God's universe without first receiving His permission. I believe that the Lord God is over all that happens in the universe.

Angel married young, with the hope of having a loving family and a bright future. Sadly, she did not marry a man who shared the same idea. He was abusive. (When one suffers in their childhood they usually come into adulthood with the same baggage.) Rejection, verbal abuse, and physical abuse are signs of someone with a control problem. Why so much control? Control is what people believe will keep them safe. (When one has been abused, the first thing they tell themselves is ... "I am not going through *that* again! *NEVER!!*") Control is passed from generation to generation through fear and manipulation. Remember, old fashioned mind control is: manipulate, to intimidate, to dominate ...M.I.D. Angel's husband had problems: alcohol problems, anger problems, and communication problems. He was a train wreck waiting to happen. Unfortunately, he had not experienced anything EVER like he was about to.

Angel and her husband had been married for a short while and decided they wanted to have children. They tried and tried, and finally went to the doctor to see what was wrong. The doctor informed Angel that she would never have children. Her body was just not capable. Years of abductions had taken their toll on her. However, she had not come "into the know" yet. She was not always aware of what had been happening to her. Being taken by aliens was not in her mind, even though it had been occurring for years. So the slap in the face from her doctor that she could not have children was just not acceptable. Angel would not take no for an answer. This visit to the doctor would only be a hurdle for her to overcome. But she would overcome it, some how, some way. After almost two months of praying, hoping and trying to get pregnant, Angel became pregnant. What a joy and excitement to know she would now bring a child into this life. Angel went home and told her whole family that she was pregnant. She went to the doctor and he confirmed it. Unfortunately from the start of the pregnancy things were different than most. Angel was a very slim lady, very small. Quite rapidly her stomach bulged and it became very hard, which made it very uncomfortable. After three months, Angel had a terrible nightmare. (At this point in her life, the abductions had not yet surfaced. What she did know was that she had had very bad nightmares. She rarely discussed these nightmares with anyone, due to the nature of their content.) After this very horrific nightmare, she woke up and found blood all over the sheets. She was quite alarmed at the sight of so much blood. Angel immediately went to the doctor to be examined. As the doctor checked her out, he said, "You're not pregnant. There's nothing there." This was devastating for Angel. She just could not believe it. Not only was her life of constant nightmares hard to cope with, now to have this added burden was overwhelming. What was going on?! She could not understand, but one thing was pounding within her soul ... She would not give up.

It had been over a year and a half since the occurrence of Angel's traumatic nightmare. She and her husband had not given up on trying to have children. Her life moved a little bit more into what *seemed* to be the norm. After almost two years of marriage, Angel once again became pregnant. And of course ... The same thing happened to her. Still very slim, her stomach started to bulge and protrude after only a couple of months. After three months she looked huge, as if she were six or seven months pregnant. People would come up and ask, "When are you due? Next month? In a few weeks?" Angel would reply, "No, I am three months along." Most people would respond, "No, that cannot be right, you're too big!" *S-T-R-A-N-G-E!* This pregnancy had *strange* written all over it. Another unusual finding was that Angel had a very high white count in her blood. She was Rh O negative. When she ate anything, she would immediately throw it back up. She could not keep anything in her stomach. She was not even able to drink water without it coming back up. After a while, she was admitted into the hospital and put on bed rest so that they could observe her condition. Immediately they gave her antibiotics because the high white count in her body meant that there could have been some infection. As the doctors looked for the infection, they couldn't find any. They sent her home.

The night before Angel gave birth, something eerie happened. Her husband was watching a television program, and Angel was tired. She went in to lay down and quickly fell asleep. Minutes later, she was awakened by the most excruciating pain she had ever encountered. Her pain was centered in her abdomen and she screamed out. Her husband heard the scream and rushed into the bedroom. She explained to him that this was the most intense pain she had ever felt. While both of them were watching her stomach, it was as if the child wanted out now. Her stomach stretched to unbelievable shapes and it was almost as if the child was turning around inside her. Her husband watched in fear and screamed with terror. They did not know what was happening. As this child was moving inside her, it was using its hand, elbow, or foot to try to break out of her. Her stomach was protruding about five to six inches away from her natural form. Her husband kept yelling, "Stop it! Stop it! You're going to kill her!" Through all the pain and trauma, Angel wondered who or what he was talking about. Was he yelling at their child ...*or what?* After his yelling, her stomach stopped moving and the situation calmed down. This entire episode lasted almost five minutes. That may not seem very long, but when you are enduring such an intense and painful situation, it can feel like an eternity! Angel was so drained from all the crying and all the pain that she quickly fell asleep. Most women experience kicks and butterfly feelings in their stomach while carrying their babies ... But not an assault to the body.

The next day she went into the hospital and gave birth to a six pound one ounce baby boy. The baby was five weeks early. A preemie. After giving birth to Billy, the doctors and nurses asked Angel to start pushing again. She was so sore and asked, "Why?" "You need to birth the placenta," the doctor replied. One of the nurses went out of the room and came back with a bowl. She commented to Angel that this bowl is what they place the placenta in. After a few minutes of pushing, something plopped out. The doctors and nurses were in awe! They put the placenta in the bowl and it hung over every edge of that bowl. They were speaking amongst themselves that in all of their time in medical history, they had never seen a placenta that big! They said they wanted to send it off to be studied. Of course, those test results weren't ever disclosed and Angel was never notified again.

Most newborns immediately want to breastfeed. Not Billy ... he wanted nothing to do with mom. Angel had to tube feed little Billy for him to eat. It didn't change Angel's attitude, she was just content that she had a little boy to love and care for.

A few days had gone by and she was feeling uneasy in her heart. Something was wrong. Even looking at her son, she could tell that something was wrong. Angel was a loving mom and her newborn boy was not attached to her at all. Every time she held him there was no response. When she went to hug him, he would literally push away. She did not understand. Angel had to deal with the fact that Billy was different.

Billy would often cry and when it came to eating, he could put it away! At a very early age, Billy was eating solid foods and a lot of it. Angel was in awe of how much food this baby ate. He was eating so much, and growing so big that she was concerned that Billy might have Sotos Syndrome. This means giant syndrome. She took him in and shared with the doctors her concerns. She began to describe that he cried all of the time. He never was satisfied. It was as if he was angry. Billy was a very aggressive little boy while growing up. He was not the huggy-lovey type. Usually when Billy went out to play, it would be just moments before some child's parent would be knocking on Angel's door. "Your child is kicking my daughter!", or "Your child is throwing sand in my son's face!" Billy did not play well with other kids. While interviewing Angel for this book, I asked her a very strong and pointed question. "Angel, was there any time when you looked into your son's eyes and wondered if he had a soul?" Her reaction was alarming. She became quiet and sort of bowed her head, and said she would share a story with me.

She began to share ...Billy was about three to three and a half years old. Angel went in to his room to check on him. It was quite late and the room was dark. As she walked up to him, his eyes were closed and he seemed to be asleep. She began to caress his head and show him affection. (This was sometimes the safest time to do this.) As Angel began to pull away, Billy immediately opened his eyes ...wide open. When he looked at his mom, she described him as looking right through her while showing her an evil smirk. Angel described his look as something right out of a horror movie. She felt like it wasn't even her son. It was like something evil was inside him, as if he had no soul. This scared Angel so much that she ran out of his room and shut the door behind her. She was devastated.

As Billy grew up, Angel had another child. She gave birth to another boy. They were three years apart. As Billy grew older, and bigger, and bigger, his demeanor did not get any better. He was still aggressive and Angel was facing the onslaught from her neighbors. One neighbor came over and said, "I don't want to tell you this, but I just hate your son. I've never hated a child before but I can't stand your son, and keep him away from my daughter!" This was being told to Angel when Billy was just five years old.

When Billy was six years, his mom gave birth to a baby girl. He now had a brother and a sister. Both pregnancies were very normal and which enhanced the fact that Billy was different. But Angel would not give up. She was determined to raise Billy in a normal household and give him everything he needed physically and emotionally. As Billy kept growing, eating, and assaulting kids (his age and younger), Angel knew she had to do something. She divorced her husband and was now a single mom trying to do what was right for Billy. She soon called her ex-husband and asked if Billy could live with him. This was very hard for her and she thought deep down that maybe a man's guidance was just what Billy needed. Billy moved in with his dad and "situations" seemed to slow way down.

Angel then began to share with me a story that she had not yet told anyone. Billy would come over and stay with her and the kids every so often. The three kids were not all that close. It always seemed like, two kids ... Plus one. One day Billy came over for a visit, which always meant staying overnight at Angel's house. That night, while Angel was sleeping, Billy sexually abused his brother and sister. Billy was only twelve years old. His brother was nine, and his sister was six. The next morning, the two children came in to mom's bedroom and shared what had happened. Social services got involved and both children confessed the horrifying details of their sexual assault. After that, Billy was placed in a children's hospital for psychiatric evaluation. After being there for one day, he tried to kill another child who was at that hospital. Angel went back to visit him, and found him in a padded room. He couldn't visit with anyone for twenty-four hours. After that time, Angel went in to visit Billy. "Are you okay?" she asked. "Oh yeah, that kid just ticked me off, so I thought I would show him a thing or two," Billy retorted. Angel saw absolutely no remorse in Billy for what he had done. She asked him if he was sorry. He immediately snapped back and said, "No! He ticked me off, I'd do it again if I had to!"

Today, Angel is "in the know". She now understands abduction and what has been happening in her life for many years. I asked Angel some more pointed questions. For instance, did she think he was completely human? Does he seem to be from you and your husband? She had a hard time answering. "I don't know." Looking back she says, "With my pregnancy before Billy, how was I just pregnant three and a half months, and then one night ... Nothing? The fact that Billy is so different. He has so much anger."

Today Billy is twenty-three years old, weighs 400 pounds, and has a height of 6'8". He wears the largest size shoes available, and if his foot keeps growing he will have to have custom shoes made. I asked Angel if he is strong. She started to giggle and said, "Is he strong?! He has the strength of six guys his age!" Billy's looks are quite different from the rest of the family. His brother and sister have dark hair and dark eyes, and Billy has blue eyes and light colored hair. He has a hard time keeping a job and has physical problems: allergies, depression, rage, and massive headaches. His headaches started, as he grew older. Some who read this will tend to lean toward the side that this boy is not a Nephilim, he's just a boy with a lot of problems. This could be ... *Or maybe not!*

Angel, having a lifetime of abductions and pregnancies confirmed by doctors, to then turn out to be false only to disappear in the night, seemed all too weird. To have a child born 5 weeks premature and have it weigh in at 6 lbs. 1 oz, is odd. Billy's own brother and sister are afraid of him. Billy does not long for the family life. He does not care about it. It just doesn't matter. It's like family and love are not built into his system.

I keep thinking about the scripture in Genesis, *"There were giants in the earth in those days; and also after that."* I also think about Dr. Jacobs' patient (an abduction victim) who is asked by the entity, "Can you see any difference in the people in this photograph? See, we can look just like you." This scenario happened to many abductees. Are we to hold on to our beliefs, or should I say *unbelief,* that literally comes against the Word of God in Genesis 6:4?

I recently found a book that gave me much enlightenment. It is called The Book of Enoch, edited by R.H. Charles. Many people believe these writings of Enoch should have been added to the canon of scripture. There is nothing found in the book of Enoch that comes against the scriptures. So why didn't it become part of the Bible that many hold so dear today? Maybe, because Enoch was an Apocalyptist. The Lord had shown him much, and what God showed him was an end that was filled with destruction. Prophets don't choose what they are shown, they just see. Prophets are often called seers. When speaking on the Nephilim, Enoch, a seer, had been shown exactly what they had been up to. On page 34 of The Book of Enoch, it states: *"And it came to pass when the children of men had multiplied that in those days were born unto them beautiful and comely daughters. And the angels, the children of the heaven, saw and lusted after them, and said to one another: 'Come, let us choose wives from among the children of men and beget us children.' And Semjaza, who was their leader, said unto them: 'I fear ye will not indeed agree to do this deed, and I alone shall have to pay the penalty of a great sin.' And they all answered him and said: 'Let us all swear an oath and all bind ourselves by mutual imprecations not to abandon this plan but to do this thing.'"*

You see, these fallen ones knew it was wrong, they knew there was a penalty, yet did it anyway. In fact, they gathered together and agreed that they would carry out this plan. Now here's where it gets wild. On page 35 of this book it says: *"And all the others together with them took unto themselves wives, and each chose for himself one, and they began to go in unto them and to defile themselves with them, and they taught them charms and enchantments, and the cutting of roots, and made them acquainted with plants. And they became pregnant, and they bare great giants, whose height was 3000 ells: who consumed all the acquisitions of men. And when men could no longer sustain them, the giants turned against them and devoured mankind."* Now listen to this next sentence and see what you get! *"And they began to sin against birds, and beasts, and reptiles, and fish, and to devour one another's flesh, and drink the blood. Then the earth laid accusation against the lawless ones. And Azazel taught men to make swords, and knives, and shields, and breastplates, and made known to them the metals of this earth and the art of working them, and bracelets, and ornaments, and the use of antimony, and the beautifying of the eyelids, and all kinds of costly stones, and all colouring tinctures. And there arose much godlessness and they committed fornication, and they were led astray, and became corrupt in all their ways."*

I was not sure what the word antimony was, so I looked it up and thought I'd share it with you. Antimony: a brilliant silvery metallic element used especially in alloys. Could this be a part of the metals in flying discs? I find it interesting how Azazel makes known to them the metals of this earth.

Enoch refers to these fallen angels as watchers. Could these watchers/fallen angels be teaching the same things and taking the same oaths today? We are always told that history repeats itself. Is the proverbial "Greada Treaty" another link to the fact that our world leaders have been taught the secrets of technology in trade for their own souls? If you were taught that there is no punishment or hell, then there would be nothing to lose. When you read the pages of <u>The Book of Enoch</u>, there seems to be as much or even more references to hell than you even will find in the Bible. Angel's story is true. How many will believe? Was the book of Enoch kept out of the scriptures because there was too much in it that exposed the watchers? Were there too many visions of hell and punishment? As you read on in <u>The Book of Enoch</u>, you will find out the penalty that comes upon the watchers and the men that have made covenant with them.

> **It is a hard concept to accept that the Nephilim were on this earth, let alone to believe that they are here now.**

It is a hard concept to accept that the Nephilim were on this earth, let alone to believe that they are here now. Have genetics been altered so much that these Nephilim look just like us? Has the enemy infiltrated our infrastructure so deeply that there is no hope? Are we to turn on our television in the near future and see evidence that the words on this page were and are absolutely correct? Maybe.

I was taught in a certain class to always be aware of your surroundings. How many people are there in the room with you? How old are they? Are they male or female? What are they carrying? How many cars are there in the parking lot? License plates ... Where are they from? Most people do not care about their surroundings. Too much "James Bond" diluting the real truth. Too much fun and games ... we become dull. I encourage you to open your eyes and become very aware of your surroundings. Natural and spiritual. Go from close-minded to open-minded. Those who dig for truth will sacrifice everything to come "into the know."

Hope is in the heart. The heart can change the course of a person's belief. The heart can change the course in the natural, and in the spiritual. Maybe this is why God looks at the heart and not our works. What is the course of your life?

NOTES

The Tenth Chapter

The Silencing of the Lambs... There's Blood on Someone's Hands

I want to start again with a statement of truth that I wish could be on every billboard across America. We are in a spiritual war. Slowly, but surely, we will have to move to whichever side we are going to stand on. We always are taught that there is black, white, and of course, there is the gray area. Most people love to live in the proverbial gray area. The gray area is where you want to stand if you always want to seem right. Not if you are right, but if you want to seem right. The gray area is the place where people who compromise stand. It is the place where one sits on the fence. It is the place where one has one foot in hell, and the other in heaven. But it is also the place of delusion and despair. If you search for the truth you will find that you cannot have one foot in heaven and one foot in hell. If you have one foot in hell, God will have nothing to do with you. That's

> **The gray area is the place where people who compromise stand.**

like working for a bank and saying you only steal money half the time you work there.

Many UFOlogists have done years and years of research, extensive research, to wind up at the end of their careers giving up. Here's the real question, did they give up, or does it just look like they gave up? Shadow governments use some of the best play actors. Let me explain why. Let's borrow Tom Cruise for a moment. He, at this time, is an A-list actor and demands the most money for acting. But if we asked Tom to do a scene for us he would immediately reply, "How do you want me to portray that scene? What emotions do you want this scene immersed in?" Tom would need a director to tell him how to act. These Shadow Government play actors need no director. Satan is the playwright. And the great and terrible day of the Lord is at hand. Great if you're on the right side, terrible if you're not. What does "at hand" mean? It is in God's Hand. He is in control. Always. Many, many people throughout the years have asked me, "Why would God cause war and kill innocent people? If God was a loving God He would not allow that to happen to us!" Hello! Wait a second! We have done it to ourselves. We rob the bank and then ask God to save us. Doesn't that pretty much sum up a hypocrite? Many don't even know that they are hypocrites. We say one thing, and do another.

I am baffled by a man who is quite knowledgeable of UFO's and such. He spent most of his life researching and putting puzzle pieces together so that we might have a better understanding of this UFO phenomenon. It is the sifting of the wheat and tares. But still the big question is... Where is the TRUTH?

Norio Hayakawa was the head of the Civilian Intelligence Network. He spent 45 years in UFOlogy. Forty-five long years with many findings and accomplishments. Let me share with you a statement made by Norio on February 4, 2005: "Con artists have peddled (and some still are peddling) disinformation, misinformation as well as down right false rumors through the Internet as well as through appearances on wacky talk shows such as Art Bell, etc. and it is amazing how some gullible segment of the population (including some so-called "UFO researchers") are taken in by these hucksters. It is no wonder that the mainstream seems to continue to categorize UFO research as part of a "pseudo science".

I have to admit that I myself spent more than 45 years of my life in this wacky world of "UFOlogy" and have nothing to show for it after all these years of fruitless pursuit of this subject matter.

However, there are many in this field who do not share my rather pessimistic view of UFOlogy. There are some sincere and honest persons of integrity in "UFO research" field.

As for me, I was at one time caught up in the frenzy of Area 51 conspiracies, etc. and made many foolish mistakes that I regret very much.

I am glad to get out of this field, although I did learn a lot about human psychology during these past 45 years."

Let's break down some of this article to get a better idea of what's going on. Does this sound like a statement of someone who devoted forty-five years of their life and passion to something they believe in? Does something sound a bit off here? Again, you might say there is a groundbreaking difference in his two statements. This is a quote from Norio taken from the book Dulce Wars, by author William Branton, around 1990. "Norio Hayakawa contends that the Grand Deception will immediately follow a rapid series of shocking, incredible events in succession, beginning with a Russia-backed Arab Confederacy's attempt to invade Israel, simultaneous worldwide earthquakes, worldwide stock market crash, and a sudden, mysterious evacuation of a segment of the planet's population, all of which will culminate in a quick official formation of a New World Order (based in Europe) that will last for seven years based upon its inception. Norio further states that the Grand Deception and the shocking series of events will put millions and millions of people worldwide in an absolute stupor for months during which time a special, extremely effective, multi-leveled "mind-control" program will be activated to calm down the stunned populace." Norio chose his words well. He used the word stupor, which means stunned or shocked or even a deep-like sleep. To me this likens to the scripture in Romans 11:8, *"According as it is written, God has given them the spirit of slumber,* (or stupor in some translations) *eyes that they should not see, and ears that they should not hear, to this day."* Could this revelation from Norio and the fact that God Himself gives them the spirit of slumber be a warning that if this event of mass evacuation was to happen we wouldn't even see it coming?!! When I found the quotes from Norio I was excited to see someone going out on a limb to state what they think could happen. All to find that after forty-five years of hard work and research, Norio has changed his view. He even gave a goofy website to go to, that made UFOlogy seem like a place to go for people who have lost their minds and cannot think for themselves. This was most disturbing to me. Why did he do this? Did someone get to him? Were there threats? The best way to find out is to go directly to the horse's mouth. Through a friend who knew Norio, I was able to contact him and ask him some very candid questions. Why did you change your position? Answer: "I didn't really change my position." Holy Cow! Are you serious?! He went from believing in a mass evacuation followed by seven years of chaos, to changing his belief that Area 51 is just a conspiracy. I asked Norio if he had ever been threatened by anyone from...? He was silent for a few seconds, then stuttered for a bit, followed by a stern, "No", a laugh, a giggle, then "No, not at all." The question lies in *what is truth?* Who or what changed a forty-five year veteran UFOlogist into believing that he was no more than a con-artist peddling disinformation?

It does not stop at Norio. How about another example of a man with quite a track record of not backing down who changed his views in the last days of his life. This man's name was William Cooper. Bill Cooper was the author of the best-selling "underground" book titled <u>Behold a Pale Horse</u>. His book carries such subjects as: The History of "Alien" Intervention, The Majestic 12 (The Truman years), Council of Foreign Relations & Trilateral Commission, Dreamland, and the New World Order Revealed, just to name a few. Bill was known by many as gruff, bold, outspoken and for being a bit of a rebel putting it mildly. He was a talk show host on short wave radio and was relatively unknown until he started blowing the whistle on the government and started sharing plans about the New World Order. He went so far as to expose classified documents that he once claimed he saw of crashed UFO's and aliens captured by the United States. He claimed that he was a Naval Intelligence Operative with top-secret clearance. He claimed that socialism was on the rise and that there would be a dismantling of the United States Constitution. Is this fact or fiction? Bill hated the I.R.S. and frequently would display corresponding documents stating how the I.R.S. was a fraud. He would state over the air that if anyone would come near him or his home in any way, he would use lethal force against them. Bill could be quite intimidating. So now the $2 million dollar question: "Why did Bill choose to change his stance on UFOlogy?" A man so stubborn, so bold, with no fear, all of a sudden changed his stand and said humbly about the subject of UFOlogy, "I was wrong and I most deeply and humbly apologize." A man who boldly came out with secrets on the Majestic 12, I.R.S., the JFK assassination, secret societies and more, bowed his head and said he deeply and humbly apologizes? If you want to buy into that, go ahead, but as for this author, I'm not buying it. Not for a second! From the many, many people I've personally talked with, Bill was never humble. I am not sure if he even knew what the word meant. People who knew him said that this was out of his character.

You can even see in his last minutes of life that you would not take down William Cooper without a fight. On November 6, 2001, Apache County Sheriff's officers exchanged fire on William Cooper's property in Eager, AZ. Deputy Robert Martinez was critically wounded in the head by **Our wonderful President George W. Bush made it perfectly legal for the lamb to do nothing against the wolf that preys on the lamb.** gunfire from Cooper. William Cooper died on the scene. What was the reason behind this tragic event? Cooper had a history of harassing local residents with deadly force, according to one report. He was also wanted by the U.S. Marshall's Service on unrelated felony charges. Mr. Cooper, one month prior, had been on his radio show challenging the government's claims about who and what had caused the destruction of the World Trade Center on September 11, 2001. Fact or fiction? Dead men tell no truths. Is it possible that we are reliving our childhood days? The bully does a bad deed and you know about it. Pretty soon the bully threatens you with your life to stay quiet. Is there a dark force who monitors who is telling what to whom?

Our wonderful President George W. Bush made it perfectly legal for the lamb to do nothing against the wolf that preys on the lamb. If you are in disbelief, just refer to our Patriot Act Bill. You will find out that you are no more than a lamb without protection or rights. The best way to make sure that no lambs make noise is to silence them. Please do not forget the other five men I previously mentioned in the book who were silenced or at the very least threatened. There are many, many more who have been threatened to be silent, so that the big bad wolf can get away with his dastardly deeds. The question rises again ... Why? Why is this happening? Why are we being visited? Not visited from another planet, but visited from within our earth. We ask why? For technology? Technology in what capacity? I'll let you peek into my opinions. . . Technology to control and to manipulate.

Let me share with you a very interesting meeting that took place in November of 1993. The shocking book, <u>Angels Don't Play This HAARP</u>, by authors Jeane Manning and Dr. Nick Begich, states a very interesting get together that was quite classified (non-public). This is a quote taken from page 152: "In November, 1993 about 400 scientists gathered at John Hopkins University Applied Physics Lab to discuss their work in developing non-lethal weapons technologies, including radio frequency radiation (RF), electromagnetic pulse (EMP), ELF fields, lasers and chemicals. The meeting was classified, and no detailed reports were ever publicly released. According to the press statements and the conference agenda (which were released) the programs developing the technologies had made significant advances. Enough advancement had been made to establish a secrecy veil and classify the conference. This conference took the whole program of non-lethal weapons a step forward by bringing the leading experts together for this event. The conference was sponsored by Los Alamos National Laboratory and focused on both military and law enforcement uses for these technologies. Dr. Edward Teller and U.S. Attorney General Janet Reno were the scheduled keynote speakers at the conference, although Reno was unable to attend. (The same Dr. Teller, "father of the H-Bomb", had sold the use of thermonuclear weapons to make deep water ports in Alaska in the early 1960's, promoted a Star Wars weapons system for the North Slope of Alaska in the late 1980's, and was now the cheerleader for non lethal electromagnetics.)

Are we getting closer and closer to technology that will change the course of civilization to doom and gloom? Or has technology already reached that point and we have not been informed based on governmental classified documents? In other words, extreme ... keep the lambs in the dark ... secrecy.

Listen to this statement made by Zbigniew Brzezkinski, Former National Security Advisor to President Jimmy Carter, as quoted on page 176 in <u>Angels Don't Play This HAARP</u>. He said, "Political strategists are tempted to exploit research on the brain and human behavior. Geophysicist Gordon J.F. MacDonald - specialist in problems of warfare - says accurately-timed, artificially-excited electronic strokes 'could lead to a pattern of oscillations that produce relatively high power levels over certain regions of the earth ...in this way, one could develop a system that would seriously impair the brain performance of very large populations in selected regions over an extended period' ... No matter how deeply disturbing the thought of using the environment to manipulate behavior for national advantages to some, the technology permitting such use will vary probably develop within the next few decades. This statement was made over twenty-five years ago, and was a precursor for what became reality in 1995."

Where did this electromagnetic technology start? Scientists and doctors unfortunately carry much pride in their fields of expertise. So when you try to propose the question - Could this technology have come from another source other than from the human/non-hybrid mind? The answer always seems to be ... "No." Could pride and accomplishment play into these answers?

Now granted, I am no scientist. I'm just a simple man who likes to put the puzzle pieces together. So let's put some revealing pieces together to see or paint a clear picture. Here we have a meeting taking place in November of 1993, with over 400 scientists and do you know who sponsored their get together? ... None other than the Los Alamos National Laboratory in New Mexico. Let me give you just a little background on the Los Alamos National Laboratory. This laboratory is one of the top U.S. research laboratories specializing in the study of the human genome. Better known as human genetics. Also, it is a vital center of the governments SDI (Strategic

Defense Initiative) research and development programs. Just about a hundred miles southeast of Los Alamos is Albuquerque, New Mexico's largest city. This is also the city that holds Kirtland Air Force Base, which by the way is located next to Manzano Storage Facility (a top-secret underground military facility where nuclear warheads are stored.) Sandia Corporation, one of the nations top-secret government contractors specializing in top military-industrial projects, is also located in Albuquerque. Of course the most frightening underground bases, Dulce, is only 95 miles northwest of Los Alamos. These 400 scientists could have picked anywhere in the world to hold their meeting. Why the Los Alamos National Laboratory? How interesting that Dr. Edward Teller, who researched anti-gravity flying discs, was a keynote speaker. And even though Janet Reno did not speak at that event, most know her background. She hates Christians and was once quoted that anyone who believes in Jesus Christ dying on a cross for their salvation is considered a cultist. Again, reminding you that these alien/demon/hybrids are anti-God and antichrist ... Maybe you can see the connection.

The Shadow Government wants to downsize this population to a mere 500,000 and they don't care how it is done. . . Just as long as it is done... In secret.

If we as people are intimidated by a dark force to silence ourselves from what we know or see, then the big bad wolf is going to get away with murder. And I truthfully and realistically mean ... *murder*. The Shadow Government wants to downsize this population to a mere 500,000 and they don't care how it is done ... Just as long as it is done ... In secret. No chaos, no civil war, just silent and deadly.

This huge spiritual war is just a bigger screenplay of what the mafia used to do in New York. If you talk, you're dead ... It's just a matter of how close you come to the truth, and how much you know, and who you know. People like Phil Schneider and William Cooper knew too, too much. I have had many who are "in the know" tell me to be careful! Again I'm just a simple man. But I will not be silenced. I will not lie down.

As to why Bill Cooper, the wild talk show host changed his views toward the end of his life; I believe he succumbed to the belief that the Shadow Government was using the UFO space/alien theme to promote One World Government. Bill Cooper would not be hoaxed. And as for Norio Hayakawa, in the early years, he had a great respect for Bill and had him speak in Hollywood. Could their friendship or shared findings have led Norio to change his views, just as Cooper did? Maybe?!! The only thought to that theory is ...It doesn't explain Genesis 6. It does not explain Jesus' words saying in Matthew 24 that in the end times it will be as in the days of Noah.

In Genesis 6 there was the mixing of genes. Natural man with supernatural entities. And the same sins are continuing today. People have been suffering from being abducted for quite some time. Spacecrafts have been seen way before the times of Roswell. Some of these spacecrafts are depicted in biblical art. Hovering in the background of a Renaissance painting of the Madonna and Child is an object

> **Spacecrafts have been seen way before the times of Roswell.**

radiating beams of light. To some people they see this mysterious object as a UFO. The detail form a fourteenth century fresco depicting the crucifixion shows a man traveling across the sky in an egg-shaped spaceship. How interesting! These ships and discs are depicted in biblical art. Was the government creating this hoax clear back in the fourteenth century before the *government* was even birthed? You see, this is just more evidence to show that the UFO phenomenon is not a hoax, but just a cover-up by some dark power that wants mankind to bow down to it, instead of the Living God.

What is going to be the stand of those researching today when they are backed into a corner? ...To compromise and shut up or to face the consequences for telling the truth. If you silence the lambs, the wolf rules the world. Does the wolf disguise itself as something other than a wolf? A very interesting book gives us that answer. The Bible states, *"Behold, I send you forth as sheep in the midst of wolves; be you therefore wise as serpents, and harmless as doves."* So another powerhouse question, are the serpent and the wolf on the same team? You decide.

ΠOTES

The Eleventh Chapter

The Media Controls Your Fear

How many people have ever watched a movie? When most viewers watch something that is unbelievable, they will laugh or scream or just stare in awe. The film industry has been faithful in getting and keeping our attention. It is one of the highest money making industries on the face of the planet. Let me explain. When you read something on paper, it can be moving, touching, inspiring, etc. But an image that you have seen on the screen or television can change the way you think. We have all heard of subliminal messages. The word subliminal means: below the threshold of sensation or consciousness. In other words, you don't know it's happening.

> There is another way besides subliminal messages to get the public to do what leaders or companies want them to do. The term is called *propaganda*

There is another way besides subliminal messages to get the public to do what leaders or companies want them to do. The term is called *propaganda*. This means organized propagation of a doctrine by use of publicity, and/or exaggeration. Now if you notice, it does not say in the definition, that the doctrine had to be true. Just a doctrine. My point is, that "media" movies and "media" news have been leading people astray for eons. And how interesting when you look up the word media you find it comes from the root word *medium*. Medium is defined as: one through which messages are sent from the dead.

We so often criticize the small reporter or investigative journalist because we don't believe them. We heckle, we slam, and we crucify the small reporter because he's telling a story that "Big Media" is staying silent about. Yet we go to town and talk to strangers about what we just saw aired on Fox News. As if Fox News was God Himself. What is the difference between small time reporters and Fox News? It's about who is popular. It was once said, "That if you tell a lie enough times to enough people, it will sound like the truth." In other words, it will be perceived as "truth". Just an interesting comment on Fox News: Do you know the definition of a fox? 1. A wild canine animal with a bushy tail and red or gray hair. 2. A cunning person. 3. Deceive or trick.

Director/Producer Robert Greenwald does a pretty good job exposing Fox News in his documentary film, "Outfoxed". How many times have you seen Fox News report on a UFO or interview someone who was abducted? They're more interested in putting out disinformation on this particular subject. This is not just to pick on Fox News, it's that they are the leaders in disinformation. Unfortunately, we feed off these media powers and believe most everything that they say. No wonder Jesus calls us "sheep".

> It was once said, "That if you tell a lie enough times to enough people, it will sound like the truth."

I travel quite often and when I pull in to have dinner or lunch somewhere, guess which station is on the overhead T.V.? You guessed right. Fox. They're not reporting news, they are reporting *F-E-A-R*. If you take a few minutes and study the network you will find that everything they report on pushes fear and has an agenda. The question is, "What, or who's agenda?" If you remember back, there was an alien autopsy filmed around 1947. This was about the same time that the 1947 Roswell crash took place. When I looked into this event, it seems that Robert Kiviat worked for none other than ... Fox. As the story is told, Robert wanted Don Ecker from UFO MAG to come aboard and be a main player in their endeavor. Fox was trying to negotiate with Ray Santilli for the rights to air it. There were rumors of Rupert Murdoch and Steven Spielberg owning footage of this film. In fact, it was a rumor Murdoch didn't own any of the footage. What is unfortunate, is when the "big chiefs" get a hold of situations like this one, it gets ugly. The story had begun with a cameraman selling the alien autopsy footage to Ray Santilli. Ray had disclosed that this was footage of the actual aliens at Roswell. Ray was wrong. The autopsy had been filmed on July 1-2,1947. The recovery had taken place in the beginning of June. This was different than the Roswell crash. As we watched this story unfold, they discovered that the saucer crashed just fifteen miles away from the White Sands Proving Grounds and the Bosque del Apache National Wildlife Resort, a former reservation. I find it interesting that discs crash near U.S. Military Bases and then ... There's a cover-up. And now, we add the media, who covers up any REAL truth that has been "uncovered".

Reporters who work for the mainstream media are paid well, and if they report anything other than what is ordered, they are fired, black balled, and so forth. The alternative media is much, much smaller. It does not reach the amount of people that the "Mega Media" can. So what we end up with is a media conglomerate who eats up its competitors if they don't abide by the rules.

Let me give you a taste of the truth from reporter Al Franken about Rupert Murdoch: "There's one important thing you should know about Murdoch, he is evil. I defer to the <u>Columbia Journalism Review</u>, Murdoch uses his diverse holdings to promote his own financial interests at the expense of real news gathering, legal and regulatory rules, and journalistic ethics. He wields his media as instruments of influence with politicians who can aid him, and savage his competitors in his news columns. If ever someone demonstrated the dangers of mass power being concentrated in few hands, it would be Murdoch." Rupert Murdoch is the owner of Fox, T.V. Guide, Harper Collins Publishing, Twentieth Century Fox, The London Times, The New York Post, and Forbes... Here's a clincher for you ... The New International Version of the Bible! We must understand the severity of being fed lies and propaganda poison, and what that actually does to change our beliefs. Fox News was one of the biggest supporters of George Bush's war in Iraq. Fox has always been supportive of the Bush's mayhems.

Let me share some facts of a few hush-hush stories that Fox did not want to share in depth. In early April 2003, our troops stationed in Iraq, launched one of their first assaults on the Baghdad National Museum. Is this a place that must be bombed and burned because of terrorists? I did not know that terrorists would camp out in the middle of Baghdad in a museum. I am not anti-American, but I must say that this travesty is sick and wrong! My thoughts on Rumsfeld with his babbling and laughing about the huge looting going on with our troops are not good thoughts. Our men were taking artifacts that date back as far as 7,000 years. According to the museum's deputy director, who blamed U.S. forces for refusing to prevent the plunder, said at least 170,000 items were taken or destroyed.

Coincidentally, at the close of the Gulf War in 1991, Iraq's Regional museums were looted by mobs and 4000 items were stolen or destroyed under Daddy Bush's watch. Also at that time, Donald Rumsfeld commented, "Stuff happens," which was told at a Pentagon news briefing on April 11, 2003. This is just not acceptable! You will not find these stories reported on by the mainstream media. The question arises, "Why knock over museums?"

Look at these parallels:

1991-Bush Sr. invades Iraq
2003-Bush Jr. invades Iraq

1991-Bush Sr. is after Sadaam Hussein
2003-Bush Jr. is after Sadaam Hussein, (even though we should be after Osama Bin Laden)

1991-Iraqi museums are hit and looted
2003-Iraqi National Museum is hit and looted

Are you seeing this? Is this coincidence? I think not. Let's not forget the favorite three letter word that all Bush babies are taught as soon as they come out of their mothers' womb...*OIL!* Worse yet, we have the media, or should I say *"medium"* covering for their unlawful acts. I repeat, unlawful acts. I believe in my heart that our troops did not knock over these museums because they were a terrorist threat. Nor did they do this because they were bored and had nothing to do. It is possible that they were ordered. And if they were ordered ... Why?

In archeological circles, Iraq is known as the "cradle of civilization". No other places in the Bible, other than Israel, have more history and prophecy associated with them than Babylonia, Shinar (Sumer), and Mesopotamia. Around the time of World War I, the British changed the name of this territory to "Iraq". Is there a reason our government is going in and desecrating the land known as the "cradle of civilization"?

There is a black market for ancient art objects. Was our government in on another scandal, or just in the middle of a huge coincidence? In January of 2003, an American delegation of scholars, museum directors, art collectors, and antiquity dealers met with officials at the Pentagon to discuss the forthcoming invasion. They specifically warned that Baghdad's National Museum was the single most important site in the country. McGuire Gibson of the University of Chicago's Oriental Institute said, "I thought I was given assurances that sites and museums would be protected." The Pentagon was warned twice more by Gibson and was sent numerous e-mail reminders to military officers in the weeks before the war began. However, a report came in on April 14, 2003, from the London Guardian stating, "Rich American collectors with connections to the White House were very busy persuading the Pentagon to relax legislation that protects Iraq's heritage by prevention of sales abroad."

On January 24, 2003, some sixty New York-based collectors and dealers organized themselves into a new group called, "The American Council for Cultural Policy", and met with the Bush Administration and Pentagon officials to argue that a post-Sadaam Iraq should have relaxed antiquities laws. Is the Bush Administration that corrupt or just always being at the wrong place at the wrong time?

The great British archeologist, Sir Max Mallowan (husband of Agatha Christie), who pioneered the excavations at Ur, Nineveh, and Nimrod, quotes some classical advice that the Americans might have been wise to heed: "There was danger in disturbing ancient monuments ...it was both wise and historically important to reverence the legacies of ancient times.

Ur was a city infested with ghosts of the past and it was prudent to appease them."

Ghosts are spirits. What kind of spirits? Fallen spirits? Is there truly a Holy War in Iraq? George Bush, our President is a Skull and Bones member and has not publicly repented for his involvement in Satanism. And of course, the media that leads to all fear, taunting, "The terrorists are coming! The terrorists are coming! Threat level today is elevated!" Here's a dandy of a question, "How do they know that the threat on the United States is elevated?" Because, *they say*. There is no proof. Bush has made some pretty radical terrorist-like comments himself. If you disagree with the President, you are considered a terrorist. That's like me threatening you, that if you don't agree with me on this book you need to be incarcerated. That's ludicrous thinking! Why didn't Fox or CNN cover Bush calling the constitution a "God-damned piece of paper"? He's the leader now and we need to follow him.

> **George Bush, our President is a Skull and Bones member and has not publicly repented for his involvement in satanism.**

The truth be known, people watch mainstream media and believe it to be "the gospel" itself. The question arises in my mind, "Could it be possible that there were artifacts, or just one artifact that was a key to opening a gateway to the fallen ones?" I know it sounds absurd, but with the way this world is changing, evil is prospering, greed is increasing, and the way Christians are sleeping, I believe it could be possible. If not, are we to say that there's another corruption in our government for the "_SOUL_" purpose of money? You see, if the media propels us into fear, we will never stand up for what's right. Don't just take my word, search and investigate for yourself. Figure out what this book is saying to you, then help get the truth out to the millions who are sitting in their homes paralyzed with fear.

Here's a study for you: Don't watch any news on television. No O'Reilly, No Hannity, No nothing! See if your fear meter goes down. Less fear ... More truth. More truth ... More courage. More courage ... More faith. More faith ...We win! You have only one life to live on this earth, make it count!!!

NOTES

Ronnie McMullen

The Twelfth Chapter

The Theory

Balance is everything in life. I remember as a kid getting on the teeter-totter, some call it a seesaw. I used to think that it was so much fun going up and down, making the other person stay up. But I soon realized that if the other person was much heavier than I was, it was not much fun at all. If you were alone you just didn't have the same desire to get on it because it didn't quite work the same. Why. . . Because you are out of balance. I find that we're all somewhat out of balance in this life. In fact, in my own life I see where even I start to slide toward one side and become unbalanced.

UFOlogy can become quite unbalanced. In the research of UFOlogy I have found some wonderful people and some who have perhaps taken it a bit too far. I do notice that in the study of UFOlogy that there is one common goal. The goal is to find out what the *truth* is behind what is going on out there.

In 1969, a non-profit organization was founded called M.U.F.O.N. It stands for Mutual UFO Network and it has over 3000 members, with Dan Aykroyd as their spokesman. Why not Steven Spielberg for a spokesman, he has done plenty of movies on the subject? I believe that there are those who want to find the truth, and those who want the truth not to be found. The more one digs for truth, the more one can find out just how ugly the truth really is.

In this book I have hit on different subjects covering the facts that these fallen ones are here and are back to their old tricks. I have talked about the Nephilim being here, and tried to show you some of the cover-ups. I wrote about the Greada Treaty that was signed with the fallen ones; where we traded our own people (who were handled like guinea pigs) for enhanced technology. We know that world leaders in their arrogance and pride are working steadily to cause this world to be conformed to their New World Order. Their goal is to downsize the population to fit their need. There will be the rich, and the slaves. Soon, there will be no middle.

As this book is coming to its close, I want everyone to know that NO, I am not a spaceship chaser. I do not have a huge fascination with aliens, and I never wanted to study this phenomenon. I did become aware in the 1990's about the corruption in our government. The shadow government was lurking, hiding its face behind a veil that would soon be removed. The days of Hitler are not over. Gary Schultz, another very thorough UFOlogist, fell into researching UFO's much like I did. When you start investigating and searching for the real truth, you start to see the connection between the New World Order boys and the UFO alien agenda. We know that the Illuminati wants to downsize the population (*murder*) so that their lives can be rich and luscious. Who are these men who chant to Satan to gain more power and wealth? If aliens could laugh they would be on the floor laughing at these men in a stupor.

The fallen ones have given enough technology to the puppet masters of this earth to make them think that they are gods. Pride, power, and wealth destroys lives. I find that as you watch people climb the ladder to power and wealth, they digress in humanity and compassion. Who are some of these men or families that have appointed themselves to be rulers or gods? They are none other than: the Rockefellers, the Chase's, the Bildebergers, and the Rothchilds. It is known to some, that these families are the controllers of our world, Presidents, and rulers of other countries. They are no more than puppets answering to a higher power. We must be aware that power always has its peak. These world rulers think they are "the peak". They have convinced themselves that they *are* god through wealth, power, fame, and pride.

I want to remind you that the Lord God has power over *ALL*. He has a divine order He has set in place and it cannot be broken. No one has the power or authority to break this divine order. The Lord God has given

Lucifer power over the world. In Ephesians 6:12 it states, *"For we wrestle not against flesh and blood, but against principalities, against powers, against the rulers of the darkness of this world, against spiritual wickedness in high places."* It is hard to understand that our so-called leaders are guiding us down the road to destruction.

Most of the public is so far out of touch that this book would read as a nightmare to them. A huge part of America strolls into "Wally World" (Walmart), buys a bunch of stuff from China that they don't need, picks up some groceries (microwavable goods and junk food), only to end up at home, sitting in front of the T.V. watching movies. Little do they know that they are handing their money over to an empire which stamps out America and endorses sweat shops in third world countries so that their profits can be astronomical. Meanwhile in the states, they built an underground compound with a heliport, landing pad, surrounded by barbed wire fencing. Why? In case of a nuclear holocaust they will remain safe to continue in their shrewd business affairs. See "The Walmart Movie", by Robert Greenwald, for a true taste of reality. "Wally World" sells all of those DVD players, televisions, stereos, electronic toys, all in the name of "capitalism". We, the public, have given "Wally World" the highest earthly honor as the largest retail giant in the world. Newscasters, when covering stories on Walmart, always refer to them as the retail giant. Call this anything you want but pretty, because every story in school that I ever read about giants, always portrayed them bringing harm to the little guy. Walmart was one of the first companies that implemented the "cool" use of the debit card machines. And we as sheep said, "That is more convenient for us! Do it! Do it! Do it!" Walmart was one of the first companies for the RFID (radio frequency identification detectors). They actually sell clothes with RFID chips embedded in the cloth. Walmart loves surveillance and tracking. Maybe they are trying to be more like our government every day. Unethical business practices of surveillance and tracking is done without the public's consent. All of this is going on while using loopholes in the system, so they don't have to pay their taxes. Yep! This sounds just like our government. It seems as if the corporate world is moving in and trying to shackle us to the concrete wall. Unfortunately, we are doing it to ourselves. Our technology and greed seem to be of more worth than our integrity.

What is now heart-breaking, is that this greed and technology have infiltrated our churches. This takes me back to a time when I attended a Sunday morning service, only to find that all the songs we sang, were being displayed using Power Point onto a huge screen with beautiful backgrounds. After the music slot, we then found ourselves looking at the screen as the pastor read one or two verses of the Bible and filled in with forty minutes of mumbo-jumbo. Most pastors do not even read from the Bible itself, they read from a Palm-Pilot in their hand because that is the way of this world. I have attended numerous pastoral conferences and prayer meetings, and the host will always communicate to the pastors, "No cell phones please." Even with this statement made, invariably during the meetings many cell phones will ring distracting the person to come away. Did they miss the request, "No cell phones please?" Did they rebel? Or, did they think that *they* were more important than everyone else? Maybe I am old-fashioned. Carrying my laptop in to a meeting doesn't make me feel any more important than the next guy. Are we to believe that if the power source is removed, we wouldn't be able to receive a message from God? It sometimes feels as if compromise and technology are one in the same. If the public cannot even find refuge in the church, then where is this world really headed? The religious leaders, just like our government, have signed on with corporate to take the money, compromise the truth, and make it look good and acceptable to the public. Worse yet, they sign God's name to it. They take scriptures out of context to uphold their wicked deeds of power, money, and corruption.

> **It sometimes feels as if compromise and technology are one in the same.**

We even have the secret society of the Masons with levels numbered that extend upward. The Masons have very much infiltrated the governmental systems of the United States, including our judges. Often in the courtroom, there is even a particular stance they make with their feet while standing, to signal from one Mason to the other. Its as if they have their own sign language. One Mason can identify another in court via this language. And of course, the Mason is set free.

The Mormons have also had much secrecy in their temples. Those who are in the lower levels of Mormonism are clueless to what sort of covenants are actually being fulfilled at the master levels. It is said that there are underground tunnels that lead directly to one or more of the Mormon temples. When we start to gather the facts, which we'll call "puzzle pieces", i.e. religious leaders, Mormons, Masons, etc., and put them together, you start to see the "Big" picture. You will also find that many of the religions seem to be compromising their beliefs as if they were signed on to the New World Order/One World Religion. Is there nowhere to turn?

Have the fallen angels' schemes infiltrated this world so heavily that we don't see the trees through the forest? Are we losing our hope? Has our religious system failed so miserably that people have actually lost hope in the Savior, Jesus Christ? Have we created so many arms of faith, beliefs, and ministries that we have now created a soul-eating monster? Are the fallen angels that smart? Or are we that stupid?

> When we start to gather the facts, which we'll call "puzzle pieces", i.e. religious leaders, Mormons, Masons, etc., and put them together, you start to see the "Big" picture.

Most of our population does not believe that we are in a spiritual war. This is not about what church you go to, this is about light vs. dark. John 3:19-21 states, *"And this is the condemnation that light is come into the world, and men loved darkness rather than light, because their deeds were evil. For every one that does evil hates the light, neither comes to the light lest his deeds should be reproved. But he that does truth comes to the light, that his deeds may be made manifest, that they are wrought in God."* It is my understanding that we have had too much powdered sugar and we are refusing to eat the meat. I am still shaking my head in awe, wondering why we believe the mainstream media who lie and sell propaganda, then turn around, shoot, and attack the one little reporter who brings in the truth? This is beyond my comprehension. Unfortunately, this is the way it is. It is my opinion that we must help the little reporter of truth to tell more people. This is much like climbing Mount Everest with a pogo stick.

The New World Order boys and the fallen angels have much in common. They can take you out, one at a time. Unity can be a great defense against them. Numbers in unity can cause both of these forces to tremble in fear. When one succumbs to fear, you are now paralyzed. We must mirror the fear that they try to seep into us. We must be light in a dark place. Remember, *"Everyone who does evil hates the light, neither comes to the light lest his deeds should be exposed."*

You're probably thinking to yourself, "What's the theory? What's the theory?" I know, I know. I have to set the stage before, or you will miss the view. As you can see, I pound the reader through the book that we are in a spiritual war. The fallen angels have traded their technology, only some technology, for humans, control, and clearance to be seen in this world. This clearance gives them just enough time to set up their "Grand Deception", right in front of our eyes. (*Note: The most professional terrorist works in broad daylight, right in front while everyone is watching.*) The fallen ones are working hard and fast on the diabolical plan. The spiritual war has been going on for quite some time. Casualties have been few, but the war is about ready to intensify beyond all possible imagination. Some of you will lose your lives in this next war. Some of you will gain your lives in this next war. This spiritual war has not yet really manifested in the natural for everyone to see. But it will. It is birthing right now as you read these words.

> *"What things are coming on this earth that will make the powers of heaven shake and the hearts of men fail because of fear?"*

The war on Iraq was the fuse to ignite the true Holy War. Iran will be the fuel to that fire. Most people believe that this war will be guns, men, nuclear, etc. I believe that there are only a few who really understand what we are about to face in the very near future. Let me share a scripture that most people pass over too fast and don't take the time to see what it really says. Luke 21:25-26 states, *"And there shall be signs in the sun, and in the moon, and in the stars; and upon the earth distress of nations, with perplexity; the sea and the waves roaring; men's hearts failing them for fear, and for looking after those things which are coming on the earth; for the powers of heaven shall be shaken."* So my question to you is, *"What things are coming on this earth that will make the powers of heaven shake and the hearts of men fail because of fear?"* If your heart fails, you die. It's that simple. I come back to the truth that most men don't want to look at. This Holy War is much worse than we can even imagine. It changes the real meaning of death. The Lord says, *"That the wages of sin are death."* If people's lives are taken before they have a chance to make things right with God, their payment will be death. Not just death in the natural, but death in the spiritual.

The time clock of life is ticking and only a few are looking at the real clock. Most people are looking at Satan's imitation clock that shows that we have lots of time before things get bad. Almost as if to say, "Take your time, don't hurry, it can wait."

Let me present my last piece of the pie before the actual theory gets presented. It has to do with the imitation clock. It actually has to do with the word "imitation". One of the ways to see Satan's weakness, is to watch everything he imitates. In other words, he has no original ideas. He is a copycat, a counterfeit, an imitator. Everything that the Lord God does, Satan comes right behind him and tries to counterfeit. Believe me, Satan is not going to come to your door wearing a red suit, knock on your door with his pitchfork, and show you his beady little eyes with horns upon his head. He will show up in your life *trying* to look like a Godly inspiration. He uses weak people who will not stand, and magically transforms them into doers of his business. Let me give you a scripture that confirms this statement. 2 Corinthians 11:13-14 states, *"For such are false apostles, deceitful workers, transforming themselves into the apostles of Christ. And no marvel; for Satan himself is transformed as an angel of light."* We have many people around the world and especially in the United States who are so turned off to the church (organized religion) that they don't want to hear about a Savior. Why? Because people who supposedly represent the Savior run around in a self-righteous attitude, judging others for not being as "holy" as they claim to be. This so-called representation of Christ makes people want to vomit. So, we now have a church losing its people faster than a man gambling his money on the roulette wheel in Las Vegas. The most depressing issue is that the church has compromised itself so much that they couldn't even find the truth if it was sitting right in front of their nose. The people of this nation and of this world are coming to a point that they are going to demand the truth. Always be careful not to shoot the man that carries the "left-field" story, for it may just be the truth. The workers of Satan are crafty, sneaky, deceitful, cunning, and disguised. Again, I reiterate, if you are not aware of your surroundings... You are toast!

Well, I have been ramping up for this huge theory for pages now. I could go on with explaining how the puppet masters (New World Order boys), are slowly killing us. I could move on to the subject of chemical trails in the sky that are dumping poisonous chemicals in our air on a daily and hourly basis. Most people don't even look up and notice this! When the Senators and Congressmen won't talk about an issue, there is usually a huge scandal or cover-up. *IT IS THE UNFORTUNATE FACT THAT FEW REALLY WANT TO KNOW THE TRUTH.* But for the few who get it, this is for you. Buckle-up and enjoy the ride. I will present the theory of what could happen, whole or in part, in the very near future. I will probably be mocked... But, oh well. For the sake of the few who believe, I will give some scriptural confirmations after I present my theory. This theory will be presented without commercial interruption. (Are we at the top of the ramp yet?)

O.K.----HERE IT IS!

In exactly what order this will take place, I do not know. Right now, as I'm writing this book, we are at war with Iraq. War with Iran is looking very possible. War with North Korea is on the back burner, but it is still a possibility. Russia does not like the United States and will be a main player in the first strike to the eagle (United States). Britain is our ally, but will not be able to protect us when we are struck. The supposed sleeping giant, China, has not been sleeping for quite some time. They are alive and scheming for the great assault and seizure of America. China has been secretly aligning with Russia in war games and such for the sake of practice. North Korea will probably be the pawn in a pre-emptive strike to the eagle. Its wings shall be plucked.

Now, here is where the tide changes. Most can believe this theory thus far. It is tangible at this point. This is now where I will enhance the view of Iraq. Iraq is a part of the old Babylonian Empire and so is Jerusalem. We now switch the view to the Holy War, which is over the rights to the land. Now let's take the microscope to an event that the world struggles with. It is the birth and the death of Jesus Christ. Jesus' life is the hidden mystery behind man's war with land. Worship God, everything's cool. Worship Jesus Christ, the Son of the Living God, King of Kings, and "them are fightin' words." The mere name of Jesus being mentioned causes a reaction in people. Jesus was born in Bethlehem and died on the hill outside of the Damascus Gate. How interesting that Bethlehem, where Jesus was born, is only six miles from His place of death. The number of man is the number six. When Jesus died, His blood was spilt outside the Holy City of Jerusalem. Jesus was the sacrificial lamb for man's sin. If this is a lie, a story, a fable, then why all the ruckus? The Holy War is about who is King! Is it Satan, is it God? Jesus, the Son of God, spilt His Holy blood right outside the Holy City of Jerusalem. Death is considered as unclean. This is why they crucified Jesus outside Jerusalem and also why Satan and his army of demons/fallen angels are so interested in Jerusalem. Jerusalem is God's Holy City, the city of God. Since the Son of the Living God spilt His blood right outside the gates of Jerusalem, the enemy will have his blood sacrifice right inside the city walls.

The antichrist will rise and take his throne in the Holy City. What people are not ready for is the manifestation of flying discs over Jerusalem. The fallen ones will appear in great numbers over Jerusalem and America. That is why we are seeing fleets of ships just like in Latin America. We see sightings of ships. One here, one there, but never fleets. I believe that the antichrist will be used to stop this attack on Jerusalem and America, or even the entire world.

Now remember that word "imitation"? Let me expound on the great pre-tribulation rapture. Many of our T.V. evangelists are pushing and selling a pre-tribulation rapture to the sheep. Some of these T.V. evangelicals are members of Masonic lodges and are of the occult of Satan. Oh, what a web they weave! These same false leaders have multi-million dollar ministries, and if a pre-tribulation rapture does not occur, they'll fold. End of story. Many of these T.V. evangelicals are tied in with Washington, pushing wars and giving people a false sense of security. These evangelists along with Washington (political) have merged as one power, guiding the sheep to their sacrificial slaughter.

The fallen ones/aliens have been dispatched to their command posts waiting for the trumpet to sound. Part of my prophetic theory is that there has to be an imitation rapture. There is no scriptural reference for a pre-tribulation rapture. Oh yes, the Lord Jesus is coming back for His people, just not before the tribulation. The tribulation, seven years of distress on the world, will be a terrible time. It is described as the time of *Jacob's trouble*. It will be the hardest time of trouble the world has ever seen. This time of distress is what complacent Christians do not want to look at. They don't believe that they will be here, because they don't want to be here. They do not want to suffer for the Name of Christ. In third world countries it is considered an honor to suffer and die for the cause of Jesus Christ. One would have to ask the question, "Are you really and truly sold out to Jesus Christ? Or, will you give me the fluff teaching of the "pan theory"?" It will all pan out in the end. The "pan theory" is for those who cannot take a stand. Why? Because they don't want to. There are times in our lives when we cry and complain so much for what we want, that God gives us what we want. I believe the Lord is going to allow a pre-tribulation rapture to snatch away the people. God's people? If they won't suffer and lose their lives for Jesus, then are they truly His people? "Justify away," I say. It won't put you any closer to the truth. If you cannot die for the cause of Christ, you are not sold out. In other words, you don't believe. What are the Words of Jesus? *" Believe on Me."* Not the Rupert Murdoch NIV translation, "Believe in Me."

Am I losing you? Shall we scream down another roller coaster hill? I believe that the false, imitation rapture is being staged right as these words are being written. God will allow the ones who are not His to be deceived.

This is why we have the warning of Matthew 24:24, *"For there shall arise false Christs, and false prophets, and shall show great signs and wonders; insomuch that, if it were possible, they shall deceive the very elect."* The word elect means "chosen".

You ask, "How will this rapture occur, and when?" I believe that this false rapture will come in the very near future. How? O.K. Here it goes. These flying discs put out a great amount of light when they descend upon the earth. There have been reports of mile-wide ships being seen. Imagine the light of a ship that has that much mass. Now imagine if many ships came together and combined all of their lights at the same time. What a bright light that would be! Would it not appear as the light of God?

As I was studying and praying one night, I found a confirmation to my theory. I really was not looking for this confirmation, but I must say, when you ask God for the truth, He is faithful to give you what you ask for. I have heard many theories and ideas through the years about the Bible, concerning UFO and aliens in different scriptures. Ezekiel's first chapter, known as Ezekiel's wheel, is one of the strongest sources besides the ninth chapter of Revelation.

Many who have been enlightened by the Spirit see Ezekiel's description of the wheel within the wheel as a spacecraft. As to the beings that man this spacecraft, there is a grim description. Ezekiel 1:10, *"As for the likeness of their faces, they four had the face of a man, and the face of a lion, on the right side: and they four had the face of an ox on the left side; they four also had the face of an eagle."* The scriptures go on to tell how they fly. The Bible says, *"... it went up and down among the living creatures; and the fire was bright and out of the fire went forth lightning."* In Ezekiel 1:18 it continues, *"As for their rings, they were so high that they were dreadful; and their rings were full of eyes round about them four."*

Could these eyes be lights or portholes to see? As you continue through Ezekiel's journey, you find the

Lord speaking with Ezekiel and telling him not to be afraid of these beings. Ezekiel 2:6, *"And you, son of man, be not afraid of them, neither be afraid of their words, though briers and thorns be with you, and you do dwell among scorpions: be not afraid of their words, nor be dismayed at their looks, though they be a rebellious house."*

Did you notice that Ezekiel's description is of a scorpion? This is the same description as found in Revelation 9:10, *"And they had tails like to scorpions, and there were stings in their tails: and their power was to hurt men five months."* This scripture was a tie-in that confirmed what Ezekiel was seeing.

But what about a scripture confirmation on the pre-tribulation rapture counterfeit? Again, everything Satan does is a counterfeit or an imitation of what the Lord has done, or will do. I now take you to Matthew 24:23-31, *"Then if any man shall say to you, 'Lo, here is Christ, or there'; believe it not. For their shall arise false Christs, and false prophets, and shall show great signs and wonders; insomuch that, if it were possible, they shall deceive the very elect. Behold, I have told you before. Wherefore if they shall say to you, 'Behold, He is in the desert;' go not forth; 'Behold, He is in the secret chambers;' believe it not. For as the lightning comes out of the east and shines even to the west; so shall also the coming of the Son of man be. For wheresoever the carcass is, there will the eagles be gathered together. Immediately after the tribulation of those days shall the sun be darkened, and the moon shall not give her light, and the stars shall fall from heaven, and the powers of the heavens shall be shaken: And then shall appear the sign of the Son of man in heaven: and then shall all the tribes of the earth mourn, and they shall see the Son of man coming in the clouds of heaven with power and great glory. And He shall send His angels with a great sound of a trumpet, and they shall gather together His elect from the four winds from one end of heaven to the other."*

I want to draw your attention to the order. This will be paraphrased. If any man says, "Here comes Jesus." Don't believe it. False preachers (Masonic men of Satan, will preach a false gospel, pre-tribulation rapture, prosperity gospel, "I am god") and deceive those who don't know and those who think they know. Then Jesus warns, *"Behold, I have told you before."* He also warns, *"When they say I am in the desert, Don't believe it."* Don't go. A lightning (a type of imitation light) is coming out of the east that will shine all the way to the west. But understand, *"So shall ALSO the coming of the Son of man be."*(Also indicates twice). Because the *true* return of Christ will be after the imitation rapture. Then the eagle monsters of Ezekiel 1:10 will gather at the carcass. Then, and only then, *"Immediately after the tribulation of those days shall the sun be darkened and the moon shall not give her light, and the stars shall fall from heaven, and the powers of the heavens shall be shaken: and then shall appear the sign of the Son of man in heaven: and then shall all the tribes of the earth mourn, and they shall see the Son of man coming in the clouds of heaven with power and great glory. And He shall send His angels with a great sound of a trumpet, and they shall gather together His elect from the four winds from one end of heaven to the other."* Do you see the false rapture? Picture –BAM—right in your face! Again, remember, Satan comes as an angel of light.

We now know that the New World Order boys want to eliminate part of the earth's population. We also know that those boys are signed on with the fallen angel/alien agenda. So how do they downsize without major chaos coming to the world? How do people disappear without a trace, without question? Blame it on God coming back for His people. It has been preached (the pre-tribulation rapture), thus, T.V. Masonic evangelicals won't lose their multi-million dollar ministries, the world won't fall into chaos, the New World Order boys get their downsizing program fulfilled, and the finale is that there are fewer people to rebel against "The Order".

And of course, the fallen ones will have new prey to dissect, study, and torture. Let us remember Revelation 9:5-6, *"And to them it was given that they should not kill them, but that they should be tormented five months: and their torment was as the torment of a scorpion when he strikes a man. And in those days shall men seek death, and shall not find it; and shall desire to die. And death shall flee from them."* Here's another subtle reminder, Luke 21:26, *"Men's hearts failing them for fear, and for looking after those things* <u>*which are coming on the earth*</u>*: for the powers of heaven shall be shaken."* These are important clues that will prepare us for the coming tribulation. I, myself, do not want to be raptured into a demon's spaceship, to feel the sting of a scorpion. I don't want anyone else to be *taken* up into those demon ships either. That is the purpose of this book.

Prosperity will not save you. Justifying the lie will not save you. Believing in the false rapture will definitely not save you! Even <u>The Book of Enoch</u> warns us of the coming tragedy. On page 73 of this book it says, *"And in those days the angels shall return and hurl themselves to the east upon the Parthians and Medes: They shall stir up the Kings, so that a spirit of unrest shall come upon them, and they shall rouse them from their thrones, that they may break forth as lions from their lairs, and as hungry wolves among their flocks. And they shall go up and tread under foot the land of His elect ones. And the land of His elect ones shall be before them a threshing-floor and a highway."* This seems to give us no hope. I will not leave you without any hope.

I want to recap real quick before the next chapter so that you have no confusion. We start with Iraq, from here it will escalate to wars with Iran, Russia, and China. Then, when all is lost, we will have our false rapture that will imitate the Messiah coming back for His people. As people are scared and full of fear (there are now fewer people to deal with), the alien ships will come down and attack our world. Remember the quote from President Ronald Reagan on September 21, 1987, "If suddenly there was a threat to this world from some other species from another planet outside the universe...Well, I don't suppose we can wait for some alien race to come down and threaten us. But I think that between us, we can bring about that realization." All of this chaos calls for a Savior. Oh... Wait...The Savior came upon the scene. Or did he? No, no, no... by this time the false rapture has been exposed by the true remnant of God. So they will try one more time to deceive the elect. Now the false prophet (the Pope or some evangelical monster) shall convince the terrorized people that the "Christ" (the antichrist sitting on his throne in the holy place) has come on the scene to put an end to the violence. People, (sheep), will bow to the antichrist on the throne as savior and king, but not the radical remnant. They know there is a real Savior on the way who will save them from this certain persecution. Some Christians (*remnant*) will be beheaded for their faith, some will be shot, and some will make it to the end.

I know that this theory sounds like it goes from bad to worse. Remember, I promised you hope. I as an author cannot give you hope. Only Our Savior the Lord Jesus Christ can truly give you the solid foundation of hope. The worse case scenario is that you will lose your life in this world to gain it in the next. Heaven awaits the righteous and there is a place prepared for those who love Him. There will be those who make it all the way through this mega Holy War. They will be the trained mighty warriors for Christ in these soon approaching end times. Do not be depressed! This is what the enemy wants. I love that saying, "You can't scare me with heaven!" Heart and attitude is only half the fight. I will let you in on a huge truth that many know, but few really grasp. You cannot fight a battle without armor. There is a defense suit. There is a safety net for those who really understand. Thirteen is a divine number. May you be divinely inspired in the next chapter. It very well could save your life.

ΠOTES

The Thirteenth Chapter

THE DEFENSE SUIT

I remember as a kid, one of my favorite television shows was "Batman". I found his mask and his cape intriguing... And of course the batmobile was just too cool for words! I was faithful to watch that show every day and hoped that batman would make it through his trials. It seemed that he was always nabbed by the bad guys, then escaped, followed by capturing the bad guys in the end. This would repeat every other episode keeping the young audience captivated. As an adult, I now view this show as comical, corny, and wonder how it ever grabbed me. When I watched that same show with its

> **I start this chapter to say that we can do something besides sit in fear.**

BAM!...BOOM!...BANG!...I almost had to grab my sides I was laughing so hard!

Many "Batman" movies have been released since the original T.V. sitcom, and I have probably seen most of them. But I must say, the debut of Chris Nolan's "Batman Begins" captivated the heart of this author once again. It portrays fighting crime that is unseen to the every day person. I find that the movie, "Batman Begins" parallels prophetic events that are coming in the near future. It also encourages the viewer to do something besides sit on their butts and complain about how everything is corrupt and wrong.

I start this chapter to say that we can do something besides sit in fear. There is a defense suit. There is a safety net from the fall. You must have a defense suit! What is the defense suit, you ask? Well, get ready my friends... its time to rock!

Again, I want to take you back to a name that causes a reaction in most people. It is not the name of God. When you say that you believe in God people are fine. But let me tell you, when you believe on the name of Jesus Christ, people go ballistic! I have found even the thought of baby Jesus in a manger, does not bother people. He is just a cute little baby lying in a manger filled with straw. People of the world can deal with that. But walk up to a person on the street and acknowledge Jesus Christ as Lord and Savior, and it will ignite into a *HUGE* problem!

I notice that the symbolic Jesus on the cross is not a bother for some people either. It symbolizes His death. People don't mind seeing Him dead. Most do not want to focus on Jesus being alive. Easter focuses more on a bunny laying eggs, than on Jesus' resurrection from the dead. Most of the churches in America are the biggest culprits of this "Easter Bunny" nonsense and its distraction from the risen Christ. Since when does a rabbit lay an egg? Satan is subtle in his holiday distractions. I have seen churches close their doors on Christmas (which by the way, is not the correct birth date of Jesus). Many churches also celebrate "harvest festivals" which imitate Halloween. I say all of this to show you the unmistakable distraction from the real deal.

I believe that this is the same deed the enemy uses against our defense suit. I know, most of you are thinking to yourselves that you already know what the defense suit is ...The defense suit is Jesus Christ. Well, you are right, but it's a little more involved than that. You cannot say, "Jesus Christ is my Savior", and call it quits. If you do, you'll be joining almost every fluff and puff Christian on this side of the Pecos. If the enemy can convince you that your defense suit is on and securely fastened, when it truly isn't, he has won the battle. Unfortunately, this represents a high percentage of so-called Christians today. They say to themselves, "I have my defense suit on"... when they really don't. If you are not wearing your defense suit, and you are not aware of your surroundings, you will be annihilated.

If you were told something by God, and did not heed the message, you must suffer the consequences. God will not save you when you have ignored His warnings. And if this is causing a reaction in you, right now, then you now know you're off. Maybe you think I'm off ...that's o.k. But my friends, wait and see, the words that God spoke will come to pass and you or your family may suffer if you don't heed His warning.

Let's take a brisk walk through some of the words found in Ephesians. I'll start in Ephesians 6:10, *"Finally, my brethren, be strong in the Lord, and in the power of His might. Put on the whole armor of God that you may be able to stand against the schemes of the devil. For we wrestle not against flesh and blood, but against principalities, against powers, against spiritual wickedness in high places."* In the first few lines of this scripture, four armies are set in place to come against YOU! They are also set to come against your family. Four armies. You are only one. The four armies are:

1. Principalities
2. Powers
3. The rulers of the darkness of this world
4. Spiritual wickedness in high places

Principality means: The position, territory, or jurisdiction of a prince. This definition opens up a whole new meaning to spiritual warfare. If this definition means a prince in charge of a territory, what prince, and which territory could Ephesians be talking about?

Remember in the book of Daniel where the Archangel Michael was detained? In Daniel 10:13-14 it states, *"But the prince of the kingdom of Persia withstood me one and twenty days: but, lo, Michael,* (the prince of God) *one of the chief princes came to help me; and I remained there with the kings of Persia. Now I am come to make you understand what shall befall your people in the latter days* (end times)*; for yet the vision is for many days."* We find the prince of Persia holding back the Archangel Michael for twenty-one days. This prince, Satan's representative, is a fallen angel standing against the Archangel Michael. A mortal man is no match for a fallen angel. Remember, this is a prince of the kingdom of Persia. What does this mean? Persia is modern day Iran. When we look at verse fourteen, *"Now I am come to make you understand what shall befall your people in the latter days; for yet the vision is for many days."* In other words, I want to show you how your people will fall in the last days. A fallen angel with a high rank (*prince*) is in charge of the territory of Iran.

The next word is powers. What is the definition of power? Webster's dictionary states: The ability to act or produce an effect, authority, a force or energy used to do work, magnification. If one of the spiritual armies we are facing is powers ... Could it be an authority that has the ability to produce an effect? i.e. the false pre-tribulation rapture?

Then we have the third army. The army of rulers of the darkness of this world. What could be the definition of this army? Is this army the fallen angels controlling and working with the New World Order boys, to bring Satan's ultimate plan into being? To deceive the elect or chosen, if it could be done? In John 14:29-30, we see a definition of the prince of this world. These verses are Jesus Himself speaking, *"And now I have told you before it comes to pass, that when it comes to pass, you might believe. Hereafter I will not talk much with you: for the prince of this world comes, and has no power with me."*

Finally, we have the fourth army- Spiritual wickedness in high places. This is Satan. Matthew 4:5 says, *"Then the devil* (Satan) *takes Him* (Jesus) *up into the Holy City, and sets Him on the highest part of the temple."* In this scripture Satan is tempting Jesus to give in and compromise. Satan wants Jesus to bow down to him. So he takes Jesus up to the high place of the Holy City. Please take note, this is not a conversation with God the Father and Satan. This is a conversation between Jesus and Satan, about authority, right smack-dab in the Holy City. This battle is still raging today. If your defense suit is not on, or only on part of the time, you will become a casualty. Your defense suit does not only fit the outside of your body, but it must be firmly attached to

> **If your defense suit is not on, or only on part of the time, you will become a casualty.**

your soul. This suit is made to protect your inner soul. Satan could care less about your outer flesh; he will only use the outside flesh to get to the inner soul, which is what he really wants to contaminate.

The intricate design of the defense suit is *SOUL-ly* built to wrap its armor around your heart. This will keep your soul well protected for the future. Most Christians have a hard time with knowing what the defense suit is, knowing how to put it on, and truly believing that it works. If you don't believe it works, it simply won't. If you don't put it on, it cannot protect you. And if you don't know what it is, you'll never find it.

We return back to Ephesians 6. Right after we are warned of these four armies that are ready to take us, we have another warning, *"To take to you the whole armor of God. That you may be able to stand in the evil day, and having done all to stand."* Now is that a jammed pack verse for us to understand?! Are you getting the context of this situation? We are warned of four brutal armies and we are now told to take up the whole armor of God, not a piece, that you may be able to withstand in the evil day. Shall we zero in on the word may; We may be able to withstand? I read that to say hopefully you will withstand the evil season. In other words, if you have your heart right, if you have the "defense suit" (the armor of God/Jesus Christ) firmly attached, and if you believe that it works. Then it will!

How many defense suits are available? Are there enough for everyone? Jesus loves all of us. The problem is that all of us don't love Jesus. It's very much like the bumper sticker, "God bless America". It should read, "America, bless God". With this problem, in effect, people are going to be slaughtered during this spiritual war.

I would like to share with you a mystery that the Lord revealed to me about John the Baptist. If you read much about John the Baptist, you will find that this man was an odd duck. If anyone wore his or her defense suit well, it was John the Baptist. John opened the door for Jesus Christ to step in. He kept preaching the unpopular words, *"Repent you, for the kingdom of heaven is at hand."* The religious leaders of that day did not like John. He rocked the boat, he made waves, and he did not conform. The Sadducees and Pharisees had a religion... John had a Savior. The people of today have religion... And they need a Savior.

As we look at John's appearance, we find that he was not one who blended. You might even find his attire offensive. Even in those days he was considered a radical dresser. There is a verse that sizes up this man's attire and diet, and shows us how peculiar he really was. Matthew 3:4 states, *"And the same John had his clothing of camel's hair, and a leathern girdle about his loins; and his food was locusts and wild honey."* Please understand, this was not a nice camel's hair blazer like today. This was probably a camel's skin, roughly cut, that might have looked quite mangy. We're talking... The man wore leather underwear! Well let me just tell you, he is more of a man than I. The religious leaders wore fine linen robes with tassels, that were even sewn with gold thread. They were

> **The Sadducees and Pharisees had a religion... John had a Savior. The people of today have religion... And they need a Savior.**

impressive dressers! I imagine that they compared much to Benny Hinn's $10,000 suit that he wears to his crusades. Some people in America do not even make $10,000 in a year's wages. History always repeats itself. So, now you can get the contrasting idea between John the Baptist and the religious leaders.

I would like to take a moment and put under the microscope the type of food that John the Baptist ate. Locusts and honey. I can't imagine going into Mc Donald's and asking for an order of locusts... *EEEEEH!* "And sir, what sauce would you like with your locusts? We have barbeque, hot and spicy, ranch, and honey." "Oh, I'll take the honey. Locusts are always more delicious with honey." That just sounds absurd!

The big question here is, why did God want us to know what John the Baptist wore? And why did God want us to know what he ate? For the Lord to record this in our map book of scriptures, there must have been a reason. The hidden mystery behind Matthew 3:4, "Locusts...and honey. Locusts... And honey." These, in my mind, are at opposite ends of the spectrum. This is like night and day. Why are there such extreme opposites in these two food items of locusts and honey?

After years of studying these alien/fallen angels, I have learned much. I also understand that I have much more to learn in the future. I don't believe that someone arrives at the perfect understanding until the Lord returns. It is my belief that we can receive partial understanding. So, I spent some time in prayer meditating about these two foods and their symbolic meanings. Locusts first show up in the Bible in the book of Exodus. These locusts come as a plague (Exodus 10:1-19). If you can, I want you to look beyond the insect. I want to show you these three verses. In Exodus 10:4-6, *"If you refuse to let My people go, behold, tomorrow will I bring the locusts into your territory. And they shall cover the face of the earth, that one cannot be able to see the earth; and they shall eat the residue of that which is escaped, which remains to you from the hail, and shall eat every tree which grows for you out of the field; and they shall fill your houses and the houses of all your servants, and the houses of all the Egyptians; which neither your father, nor your fathers' fathers have seen, since the day that they were upon the earth to this day."*

Now we find locusts showing up in the book of Leviticus where the Lord is giving His law on which foods are permissible to eat, and those that are unclean. Crazy enough, locusts show up as one that is permissible! In Leviticus 11:22 it states, *"Even these of them you may eat; the locust after its kind, and the bald locust after its kind, and the beetle after its kind, and the grasshopper after its kind."*

Moving right along to the book of Deuteronomy, we discover the Lord warning us that if we do not heed His Word and obey, that there will be consequences that play out. This is not a fun page in Deuteronomy 28:38. Let's zero in on the verse: *"You shall carry much seed out into the field, and shall gather but little in; for the locusts shall consume it."* Skipping to verse 42, *"All your trees and fruit of your land shall the locusts consume."* Now I'll show you the next few consecutive verses that say something in code that is very *strange*, verses 43-45, *"The stranger that is inside you shall get up above you very high; and you shall come down very low. He shall lend to you, and you shall not lend to him; he shall be the head* (chief) *and you shall be the tail. Moreover all these curses shall come upon you, and shall pursue you, and overtake you, till you be destroyed; because you hearkened not to the voice of the Lord Your God to keep His commandments and His statutes which He commanded you."* Don't you find this to be a wild scripture? What does the stranger inside you mean? I believe this could mean that there is a demonic control that you may be indebted to. This control becomes high above you, and you become very low. He shall lend to you, and you shall not lend to him. Is this our banking system, credit and debt institution, that will put all who have partaken of greed into bondage? In other words, the mark of the beast? This is when you will be marked by the New World Order boys, so that they can trace or track you every time you buy and sell goods. He shall be the head and you shall be the tail. Have you noticed the debt of our nation? It enslaves most people including Christians. Greed and money have been our distraction so that the alien agenda can move forward full steam ahead. Of course, our technological toys keep our eyes off of what is really going on.

You will also find the locusts showing up in the book of Joel, being used in the context of devouring. This is yet another analogy of a curse.

And now we shift gears to the last book of the Bible, Revelation. Before we read this take note of THESE locusts, they are no ordinary locusts! Revelation 9:2-3 states, *"And he opened the bottomless pit; and there arose a smoke out of the pit, as the smoke of a great furnace; and the sun and the air were darkened by reason of the smoke of the pit. And there came out of the smoke locusts upon the earth: and to them was given power, as the scorpions of the earth have power."* Skip over to

verses 7-11, *"And the shapes of the locusts were like to horses prepared to battle; and on their heads were as it were crowns like gold, and their faces were as the faces of men. And they had their hair as the hair of women, and their teeth were as the teeth of lions. And they had breastplates, as it were breastplates of iron; and the sound of their wings was as the sound of chariots of many horses running to battle. And they had tails like to scorpions, and there were stings in their tails; and their power was to hurt men five months."* Here is the clenching verse, *"And they had a king over them, which is the angel* (fallen) *of the bottomless pit, whose name in the Hebrew tongue is Abaddon, but in the Greek tongue has his name Apollyon."* Apollyon is translated as destroyer. This is not a pretty picture. Do you think that these are really little bugs? Or maybe... Aliens/ demons/fallen angels? Or...?

Let's view the honey. We find honey coming into the biblical picture in Exodus3:8 saying, *"And I am come down to deliver them out of the hand of the Egyptians, and to bring them up out of that land to a good land and a large, to a land flowing with milk and honey; to the place of the Canaanites, and the Hittites, and the Amorites,* and the *Peruzzites, and the Hivites, and the Jebusites."* The land of milk and honey is mentioned again in Joshua 5. In 1 Kings 14, honey is presented as a gift. We find the Lord leading and training Jacob in Deuteronomy 32, and giving him honey to suck right out of a rock. Do you like wild honey? Let me give you a taste of wild honey. The story of Samson is one that is close to my heart. Samson, you might say, was a superhero by God. Samson was the man with wild honey. Judges 14:8 says, *"And after a time he returned to take her, and he turned aside to see the carcass of the lion: and, behold, there was a swarm of bees and honey in the carcass of the lion."* Samson had been challenged by a lion. He slew the lion, visited with a woman, and after time honey was produced in the lion.

The next search for honey was quite enlightening. Now, Jacob's name was changed to Israel. Jacob fathered twelve tribes. Israel is the name for God's chosen people, and they are not necessarily Jewish. Israel is not a Jewish religion. Israel represents the remnant people who call on the name of God. And...if you don't recognize God's Son Jesus, then you do not know the Father. So again, I reiterate, Israel is not about the Jews. Israel is about the remnant. This is an important fact to know before I show you this next scripture.

There is a record of a battle between the Philistines and the Israelites in 1 Samuel 14:23-30 says, *" So the Lord saved Israel that day: and the battle passed over to Bethaven. And the men of Israel were distressed that day: for Saul had bound under oath the people, saying, Cursed be the man that eats any food until evening, that I may be avenged on my enemies. So none of the people tasted any food. And all they of the land came to a forest; and there was honey upon the ground. And when the people were come into the forest, behold, the honey dropped; but no man put his hand to his mouth: for the people feared the oath. But Jonathan heard not when his father charged the people with the oath: wherefore he put forth the end of the rod that was in his hand, and dipped it in a honeycomb, and put his hand to his mouth; and his eyes were enlightened. Then answered one of the people, and said, Your father straightly charged the people with an oath, saying, Cursed be the man that eats any food this day and the people were faint. Then said Jonathan, My father has troubled the land: see, I pray you, how my eyes have been enlightened, because I tasted a little of this honey. How much more, if only the people had eaten freely today of the spoil of their enemies which they found? For had there not been now a much greater slaughter among the Philistines?"* Verse 31, *"And they smote the Philistines that day from Michmash to Aijalon: and the people were very faint."* Did you notice when Jonathan ate of the honey his eyes were "enlightened"? What does this say about honey? What is God saying that honey means? I find interesting the science behind bees flying. They have the same propulsion system as the flying saucer (see Stan Deyo's 2006 DVD, "How Spaceships Fly").

Here is what I believe is the mystery of John the Baptist's locust and honey diet. Locusts ... Then honey. The locust represents the alien/fallen angel/demonic forces. The honey represents the reward after the battle. From crossing over to the land of milk and honey to the lion (representing the enemy) having a reward in its carcass, to Jonathan's eyes being enlightened. Funny how he put his spear in the honey to eat. Honey is the reward after consuming the locusts. You cannot consume the locusts without the defense suit.

In Ephesians 6:14 there is a little mystery that I thought I would reveal to you. The Bible says, *"Stand therefore, having your loins girt* (belted) *about with truth, and having on the breastplate of righteousness."* John the Baptist had a leather girdle belted about his loins. I believe this was and is symbolic. I looked up the definition of loins, and there it was! Loins can be defined as reproductive organs. The mystery defined here, is that our seed must be pure. It is part of our defense suit. We cannot be a part of the hybrid

Nephilim. We must be perfect in our generations, just as Noah was. Prophets see the future. And there is nothing they can do about it.

John was a prophet and foresaw the coming of the Messiah. And he was making the proper preparations. We too, must know that the Messiah is coming soon. We must engage the enemy to be rewarded with the Lord's honey. Maybe our governments know about this enemy, or maybe they don't. There are some men in strategic secret places who are God-fearing, Jesus Christ-serving men. Pray for them. Most of America will not engage the enemy for fear. But let me warn you, you cannot engage the enemy without the defense suit. You cannot win without the armor of God/Jesus Christ.

This reminds me of the western movie, "Tombstone", starring Kurt Russell and Val Kilmer. At the end of the movie, all the good guys and bad guys have been sifted down to just three men. Wyatt, Doc Holiday, and the very wicked Ringo. Doc is bed ridden and cannot fight anymore (watching the movie might give you a better visual). Doc is the fastest gun and is known throughout the territory as being deadly quick with his weapon. Ringo, the untamed outlaw, is equally as quick as Doc. The intensity builds as the end closes in. Wyatt is the law, and Doc, his friend, is on his death bed. Wyatt now knows that Doc is too sick to fight Ringo, and knows that he must engage the very deadly gunslinger on his own. As the movie thrusts forward to the climax, Wyatt asks Doc a very intense question. "Can I take him?" Wyatt asks. "No." whispers Doc laying on his deathbed. "I didn't think so," replies Wyatt in a disappointed and broken voice. In the next scene, you find the miracle of Doc confronting Ringo and egging him into a duel. Ringo states he has no quarrel with Doc. The fight takes place and Doc is victorious. Wyatt now shows up on the scene and is in awe that the fight has been won. To me, the three characters shown here parallel Jesus Christ, the enemy Satan, and ourselves.

We cannot take on the enemy. Jesus doesn't want us to be a coward. The Lord Jesus will fight our fight and confront the enemy for us. He will go before us and make our paths straight. The Bible says, *"The battle belongs to the Lord."* The defense suit is our safety net. We must consume the enemy to be rewarded with honey. We must have our defense suit on (the armor of God/Jesus Christ) to overcome the enemy and believe that it works. We must put on the armor of God so that we are able to stand in the day of evil. We can't beat the fallen ones without it. If you do not have it, you need to find it before it's too late.

The spiritual war is set in place and the curtain is about to open. Men's hearts will fail them for fear in the opening hours. This book is to warn you and to prepare you. Jesus, the defense suit, can save you. Do you have to believe me? No. But if you have read this entire chapter, whether you accept the defense suit or reject it, you will remember it in the day of trouble. It is my heart that everyone be saved. I know that will never happen, but it is still my hope. If you are in agreement, please do your part in helping with the distribution of this book. If you strongly disagree, please pray with an open heart, for there will come a day when man shall see these warnings come to pass. It is my opinion that on every cake you need icing. If you want to receive your free defense suit, please continue.

There are some interesting finds on the fraction 1/3. In the next and last chapter I will define them. You will be given the opportunity to receive your defense suit if you don't have one. The true warrior *must* proceed. The true warrior *must* finish with valor. The question is... Are you a true warrior?

�041OTES

The Thirteenth & A Third Chapter

Few Will Make It!

I know you are thinking to yourself, "This is the fourteenth chapter, not the thirteenth and one third. *You can't do this.*" Well, much to everyone's surprise, I did!

This reminds me very much of 9-1-1. There is much debate in the United States as to what really happened on September 11, 2001. In fact, it is called a conspiracy theory. This book will be noted as the conspiracy theory book. I warn you to take an educated look. First, we must look at the word *conspiracy*. It means a secret plan to commit a crime; plot. The word *theory* means: supposition or system of ideas explaining something especially one based on general principles. My question to you is, what happens when theory turns to fact and then all you have left is a conspiracy? I am not going to go into the depth of the collective facts that start proving 9-1-1 *is* truly a conspiracy.

There are two statements made by George W. Bush that admit guilt in hiding the real truth:

> 1."Let us never tolerate outrageous conspiracy theories concerning the attacks of September 11th. Malicious lies that attempt to shift the blame away from the terrorists themselves, away from the guilty."

Notice the content of this phrase. I focus on the words, "shift the blame". I believe this is not about blaming, but who the perpetrator was in the event of 9-1-1. *Terrorist* is a catchall word that could imply anyone. The terrorists became Al-Qaeda and supposedly Osama Bin Laden was their leader. Then explain why he was not captured and Sadaam Hussein was. The same Sadaam that Daddy Bush chased.

2. "Every nation in every region now has a decision to make. Either you're with us or you are with the terrorists."

What kind of manipulating statement was that? In other words, if you don't sign on to everything that the President, the Congress, and the Senate push, you will be considered a terrorist. Sounds like we have a leader very similar to what Germany had in World War II.

These statements from President Bush show that he undoubtedly has an agenda. Most people help the President to continue justifying his behavior. But, let's just wait, the enemy will always give his position away.

9-1-1 was an inside job. A great DVD to see, the real truth is "9-1-1 In Plane Site" (which I know for fact has come under a tremendous amount of persecution.) Dave Von Kleist does an awesome job of presenting the facts. I find that even when presented with all of the facts some people will still deny it as truth. The big question is, "Why 9-1-1?" Why would our government be a part of something so sinister?

Why were they also involved with the Oklahoma City bombing? The Oklahoma City bombing was the fuse to ignite fear all over the United States. Who was our President during that American tragedy? Ohhh That's right. Bill Clinton. The same Bill Clinton who helped Daddy Bush raise money for the Tsunami relief. They're golf buddies now. Do you really think that Indonesia is getting paid? If the New World Order boys are embezzling $27.5 trillion from the United States of America, (*See the Leo Wanta story, The $27.5 trillion dollar man on www.arcticbeacon.com*) do you think that they have any remorse for the 9-1-1 incident? Don't forget 9-1-1 brought us The Third Reich. Oh, I'm sorry, I meant Homeland Security. 9-1-1 also brought about The Patriot Act, which removed and violated all of our freedoms as a nation. Most of the public do not care and do not know what we've really lost. They have not read The Patriot Act, and ... they won't.

September 11, 2001 ushered in a new wave of fear for America. It was the beginning. This was the door to the great Holy War. 9-1-1 was the turning point of America as we know it. It was the beginning of the end.

This takes me to the number of this Chapter 13 1/3. I believe 13 is a divine number and I believe there is a meaning behind the fraction 1/3. There were the twelve tribes of Israel and one God, thirteen. There were the twelve disciples and Jesus, thirteen. Twelve jurors, one judge, thirteen. And so on.

Few people delve into the fraction 1/3. First let's start with Matthew 7:14, *"Because narrow is the gate, and narrow is the way, which leads to life, and few there be that find it."* I would like to show you a simple little find. Our number system is built on the number ten. So, if I had ten men standing in a room, and told you that you could use a few of those men to build your new house, how many would come with you? Three. Two is a couple, and five is half. You would probably take three, just about a third. Could it be possible that a third of our earth's population will find , *"that narrow way that leads to life which is heaven."* Not a strong enough find? O.K. O.K. Let me give you another dose of 1/3. It says in the Bible that when you receive Jesus Christ as Lord and Savior your name will now be written in The Lamb's Book of Life. If your name is not recorded there, just forget about entering into heaven. This is the Great Judgment. This is it. No second chances. It's your choice either entering into hell, **Your best life now might just cost you your best life later.** or entering into heaven. Your best life now might just cost you your best life later.

Let us peek into the future. Revelation 20:12-13 says, *"And when I saw the dead, small and great, standing before God; and the books were opened: and another book was opened which is the book of life: and the dead were judged out of those things which were written in the books according to their works. And the sea gave up the dead which were in it; and death and hell delivered up the dead that were in them: and they were judged every man according to their works."* If you notice, the *books* which recorded the wicked, were opened. *"And another book was opened which is the book of life: and the dead were judged."* So, we have the *books* full of people who rejected God, and the *book* (singular) with the names of the saved. The word *books* (plural) implies that there is more than one. So let's just say that it means two books. It could mean more. But just for the sake of it all, let's say *books* means two. So, we have one book of the names of those who are saved, and two books of those who refused Jesus. That is a total of three books. That's one third of the people who will be saved. This is the best case scenario. If *books* are equivalent to more than two, the fraction changes and less than *few* will enter heaven and see the Lord.

The fraction of one third is used in this next verse to purify and purge the people to repent for their rebellion. Revelation 8:6-12, *"And the seven angels which had the seven trumpets prepared themselves to sound. The first angel sounded, and there followed hail and fire mixed with blood, and they were cast upon the earth: and the third part of trees was burned up, and all green grass was burned up. And the second angel sounded, and as it were a great mountain burning with fire was cast into the sea: and the third part of the sea became blood; And the third part of the creatures which were in the sea and had life, died; and the third part of the ships were destroyed. And the third angel sounded, and there fell a great star from heaven, burning as it were a lamp, and it fell upon the third part of the rivers, and upon the fountain of waters; And the name of the star is called Wormwood: And the third part of the waters became wormwood; and many men died of the waters, because they were made bitter. And the fourth angel sounded, and the third part of the sun was smitten, and the third part of the moon and the third part of the stars; so as the third part of them was darkened, and the days shown not for a third part of it, and the night likewise."*

The fraction of 1/3 is not looking very promising! Don't forget the defense suit. I know that the defense suit is looking better and better to you all the time. As you read the book of Revelation, by the time we enter into Chapter 9:17-18, the times of trials and tribulations of this world are at an all time high. *"And thus I saw the horses in the vision, and them that sat on them, having breasplates of fire, and of jacinth, and brimstone: and the heads of the horses were as the heads of lions; and out of their mouths issued fire and smoke and brimstone. By these three was the third part of men killed, by the fire, and by the smoke, and by the brimstone, which issued out of their mouths.".*

Some would say by these atrocities that Jesus is mean and does not love His people. I believe those who carry this belief are filled with hurt, rejection, unbelief, abandonment, lies and blindness. I have only read a few books with the courage to tell people the real truth. Most authors just want to be famous and rich. This book will probably never hit the New York Times Best-Sellers list. Truth and reality are never popular. My reason for writing this book is: to let people in on the truth about the coming tribulation, show that these aliens/fallen angels mean business, help people to know Jesus, and to obey God on a task that was far above my means. That task was to author this book. I don't care what people think of me, I got over that

> **To wear the defense suit you must sign on to an army that is far superior than any worldly organization known to man.**

hurdle many years ago. *Please man, or please God.* Those who try to please man end up miserable. Jesus was not popular. John the Baptist was not popular. And I will not be popular. Mockery and persecution are a part of the walk on the narrow road, yet *...few find it.*

I want to close with a simple invitation, a true and honest invitation to be a person of honor and integrity, and wear the defense suit. To wear the defense suit you must sign on to an army that is far superior than any worldly organization known to man. You must sign on to the army of God, with Jesus Christ as your Lord and Savior.

You will not be kicked out with your first mistake, you will not be rejected, you will not be abandoned, and the worldly pay is terrible. I know that Joyce Meyer is telling everyone that God wants you to be rich, but that is her justification because the fact is that she is rich. She is choosing to have her best life now. Unless she loses her life in the world now, she cannot gain her life in heaven. You must be born again (your life must be changed spiritually). When I say that the pay is terrible when you sign on as a warrior, I want to let you know that the benefit package far outweighs the worldly money. Don't make a commitment you're not going to keep. Open your heart, pick up your head, and receive the defense that will make *you* the winning warrior that you're called to be. There is no better high on this earth. If you want the suit that is absolutely free, here are the words to sign on:

Heavenly Father,

I have sinned against You. I repent for my ways and ask You to change me right now in Your sight. I am tired of the road I have chosen. Lord, please forgive me, cleanse me, renew me, change me, and enlighten me, so I see this world as You do. Cause me to open my heart and love, and have compassion on others who have been hurt. Cause me to lose my anger and replace it with joy, for the joy of the Lord is my strength. I acknowledge You Jesus, as my Lord and Savior. I know and receive You dying on the cross at Calvary for my sins, and rejoice in knowing that You rose on the third day to beat the devil to prove that You are Lord. Lord, I make a covenant with You, to serve You as long as I live and receive Your direction and Your will for my life right here and now. I thank You, I praise You, and shed my shame, for I am renewed and counted in Your heavenly army. Fasten my armor oh Lord, and give me Your vision. I thank You and praise You and give You all the glory for this covenant that I have made with You. I love you Lord.

Amen.

Signed: _____

Dated: _____

If you don't sign and date this it means nothing. Be of courage and follow your heart. If you have made this covenant then I welcome you to a new life. As a God Seal (much like a Navy Seal with more rank), you will encounter the enemy in hand to heart combat. Always be aware of your surroundings. Welcome to the Lord's Army. And by the way, if you truly made covenant with God and signed and dated this covenant, your name is now recorded in the Lamb's Book of Life. You will be one of the few on that narrow road. The enemy will come at once and try to push you off. Don't forget, the Lord fights your battles. Just pray for His will.

I hope you have enjoyed this book and I look forward to meeting you ... if not in this life then in the Lord's heavenly kingdom. May you fight the good fight with power and authority.

God's Speed to You,
Ronnie McMullen

Ronnie McMullen

ΠOTES

Funny Things That Happened While Writing This Book!

I thought I would share a couple of interesting truths that took place while writing this book. You might say that this is the place where you watch the bonus scenes on your new DVD. So just think of this as the bonus material of the book.

I start with a small funny thing while I spent time writing in Eagle's Nest, New Mexico. I was grinding away when I decided that I needed to take a break. So, I took a walk down a street nearby. It was quite dark outside and I noticed directly across the street there was a fence with a gate. The gate was built with two arrow-like iron spears that were crossed. The words that were written directly over these spears said *Warriors Mark*. This was a confirmation that I had made the right decision to stand for the truth no matter what the cost.

Another interesting situation happened when I was writing the chapter about Angel. I was in the midst of writing the section about her stomach, where the baby was stretching and causing her intense pain. As I was writing I immediately received a sharp pain to my abdomen and found myself doubled over in the chair. My eyes became blurry and I grabbed my stomach wondering what was happening. I had to stop writing because the pain became too severe. As I was resting on the bed and began to pray, I was quickened in my spirit that this was a frontal assault by the enemy. The enemy was threatening me. For some reason when our physical body is attacked what is really important loses its focus. If we focus on fear, it will paralyze us. I began to praise God and then fell asleep. I woke up with a bad stomach ache but felt much better. I went to the desk and finished the task. Through the Lord I conquered this battle.

The last story I have to share changed and increased my faith tenfold. It deals with wearing the defense suit to stand against the enemy's intrusion of taking people against their will. I have spoken and literally preached on how the defense suit (armor of God/Jesus Christ) will protect us from these fallen ones taking us. I had not come across any hard evidence. I just knew this to be true in my heart. That is ... *Until Now!* One of the abductees I have been working with is truly a wonderful person. I have often wondered "Lord, how come this person was taken?" The Lord knows the answer to every question that is asked of Him. He chooses the timing when He shares His answers.

As I was talking to this person on the phone, they began to share with me that every three years the fallen ones had come to take them against their will. Each time they would perform more physical testing which was always very painful. It was about time once again for this person to be taken. Every time the fallen ones came, this abductee would hear a buzzing or ringing in their ears. They told me that the ringing had started and that they knew they were about to be abducted again. This was when I began to share with them about Jesus, and how He is the way to the Father. This individual knew God, but did not realize the strength of the Son of God, Jesus Christ. My friend prayed and accepted this truth into their heart. When the marked date came for this person to be taken, IT DID NOT HAPPEN! I repeat, *IT DID NOT HAPPEN!*

This put such a joy into both of our hearts. We rejoiced. The defense suit was tested and it worked. This is powerful! There is hope for abductees and explanations why *"things"* are taking place. Abductees do not need more havoc, they need compassion, truth, and answers. They do not need some high and mighty individual with a doctorate to tell them that nothing is really happening.

I make a statement to the ones who have been abducted against their will: I understand, not fully because I don't believe I have ever been taken. But the Lord has shown me some insight to help you. If you need help contact us and we will try to help you in any way we can. Sometimes, things are stolen from us. Life is too short to let it keep happening.

References and Sources

All scripture quotations are taken from the Holy Bible, KJV Easy Read.

William Branton- The Dulce Wars, Global Communications, 1999

Travis Walton- www.geocities.com

Artwork by Julian Finch- www.alienart-thvisitors.co.uk

Agent Wolverine- *The Underground Nazi Invasion of the United States,* www.sauderzone.com

The New American Desk Encyclopedia, Third Edition, 1994

The Merriam-Webster Dictionary 2004

William Cooper- Death of a Conspiracy Salesman, 2002

The Prophetic Watch Radio Show- Norm Franz Interview, 8/9/04 – 8/13/04

The Georgia Stones- www.radioliberty.com/stones.htm

Dr. Cathy Burns- Mormonism, Masonry, and Godhood, 1997

Phil Schneider-*Deep Underground Bases and the Black Budget*

Underground Bases- www.anomolies-unlimited.com

Compiled by "The Group" Edited by: "Branton"-*The Secrets of the Mojave*

UFO Cover-up: Art Bell Interview of John Lear, 11/2/03 – 11/3/03

The Prophetic Watch Radio Show- Interview with Stan Deyo, 1/25/06

Denver International Airport- www.anomolies-unlimited.com

Dr. Nick Begich and Jeane Manning- Angels Don't Play This HAARP, 2002

Phil Schneider- www.subversiveelement.com, www.ufodigest.com

Lockheed X-22A- www.stealthskater.com/Documents/Boylan_10.doc

Roswell Crash- www.history.navy.mil/faqs/faq29-1.htm

The Prophetic Watch Radio Show- Interview with Dr. David Jacobs, 6/26/06 – 6/30/06

Congressional Criminals- www.renaissancemag.com

Graham Conway- 2006 Denver UFO Interactive Conference, Interview 7/2006

R.H. Charles (editor)- The Book of Enoch, The Book Tree, 1999

Norio Hayakawa- www.hometown.aol

Robert Greenwald- www.disinfo.com

www.ufocasebook.com

www.virtuallystrange.net

Bush On the Constitution: *"Just a goddamned piece of paper"*- www.capitolhillblue.com

Stan Deyo- "How Spaceships Fly", 2006 Denver UFO Interactive Conference DVD, www.soldoutwarning.com

Greg Szymanski- *Leo Wanta Story*, www.arcticbeacon.com

9-1-1 In Plane Site Dave Von Kleist, The Power Hour

DVD's available at www.soldoutwarning.com or www.theprophticwatch.com:

Phil Schneider
Stan Deyo
Corina Saebels
"9-1-1 In Plane Site"
"Outfoxed"

Ronnie McMullen is available for speaking engagements and personal appearances. For more information contact:

Ronnie McMullen
Advantage Books
PO Box 160847
Altamonte Springs, FL 32716

If you would like to know more about the TRUTH listen to "The Prophetic Watch" Radio Show- Visit: www.theprophticwatch.com for times and frequencies. You can also visit our online store at www.soldoutwarning.com

To order additional copies of this book or to see a complete list of all **ADVANTAGE BOOKS™** visit our online bookstore at:

www.advbookstore.com

or call our toll free order number at: 1-888-383-3110

BOOKS & MUSIC

Longwood, Florida, USA

"we bring dreams to life"™
www.advbooks.com

Printed in the United States
65392LVS00008B/217